Making it in Sales

A CAREER GUIDE FOR WOMEN

Mary J Foster with
Timothy R V Foster

KOGAN PAGE

First published in 1993

Apart from any fair dealing for the purposes of research or private study, or criticism or review, as permitted under the Copyright, Designs and Patents Act, 1988, this publication may only be reproduced, stored or transmitted, in any form or by any means, with the prior permission in writing of the publishers, or in the case of reprographic reproduction in accordance with the terms of licenses issued by the Copyright Licensing Agency. Enquiries concerning reproduction outside those terms should be sent to the publishers at the undermentioned address:

Kogan Page Limited
120 Pentonville Road
London N1 9JN

© Mary J Foster and Timothy R V Foster 1993

British Library Cataloguing in Publication Data

A CIP record for this book is available from the British Library.

ISBN 0-7494-0953-3

Typeset by Books Unlimited (Nottm), Sutton-in-Ashfield, NG17 1AL
Printed and bound in Great Britain by Clays Ltd, St Ives plc

Contents

Foreword 9

1. **Why choose selling as a career?** 11
   Breaking out of the box 11; Advantages of a sales career 12; Tina Tietjen, Video Arts Ltd 12; No experience required 13; The secretarial start-up 14; Audrey Chessell, Austrian Airlines 14; Women in sales 16; Women *vs* men 17; Patricia Leach, Frost & Sullivan 18

2. **Know thyself** 21
   Positive traits evaluation chart 21; Negative traits evaluation chart 22; More positives 23; More ratings 24; What do you want to sell? 25; Lisa Barnwell, Café Royal 25; Making a choice 27; To whom/how do you want to sell? 28

3. **What is selling? Understanding the opportunities** 29
   Types of selling 29; Cathy Rowan, independent consultant 29; Selling in spite of the title 31; Ways of selling 32

4. **Direct sales** 35
   Typical areas 35; Qualifications 36; Customers 36; Tasks 36; Compensation 36; Lifestyle 36; Attributes required 37; Transaction time 37; Whom do you know to talk to about direct selling? 37; Sample direct sales job advertisement 38; Real-life experience 39; Betina Birtchnell, Helm Financial Services Ltd 39; Elizabeth Ayles, Howard Cundey & Company 40

5. **Multi-level marketing (network marketing)** 45
   What is multi-level marketing? 45; Complaints 47; Common questions about MLM 47; Legislation 48;

Finally 49; Typical areas 50; Qualifications 50; Customers 50; Tasks 50; Compensation 51; Lifestyle 51; Attributes required 51; Transaction time 52; Whom do you know to talk to about MLM? 52; Sample MLM advertisements 52; Real-life experience 52; Joy Fahey, Cabouchon Ltd 52; Rosie Ward, National Safety Associates 55

6. Retail sales   57
Typical areas 57; Qualifications 58; Customers 58; Tasks 58; Compensation 59; Lifestyle 59; Attributes required 59; Transaction time 59; Whom do you know to talk to about retail selling? 59; Sample retailing job advertisement 60; Real-life experience 61; Annie Marchant, Wenderton Antiques 61; Alison Kaye, Kogan Page Ltd 63

7. Telephone sales   65
Typical areas 65; Qualifications 66; Customers 66; Tasks 66; Compensation 67; Lifestyle 67; Attributes required 67; Transaction time 67; Whom do you know to talk to about telephone selling? 68; Sample telephone sales advertisement 68; Real-life experience 68; Stephanie Foster, Hazardous Materials Management 69

8. Business-to-business sales   71
Typical areas 71; Qualifications 73; Customers 74; Tasks 75; Compensation 75; Lifestyle 76; Attributes required 76; Transaction time 76; Whom do you know to talk to about business-to-business selling? 77; Sample business-to-business job advertisements 77; Real-life experience 78; Kate Charters, Reuters Television Ltd 78; Collette Murney, MacEurope Ltd 80

9. What are the compensations?   85
Straight salary 85; Salary plus commission 85; Straight commission 86; Taxation 88

CONTENTS

10. **Getting ready**   **89**
    The importance of self-confidence 89; Understand what you're worth 90; The importance of networking 91; The importance of a mentor 93

11. **Training**   **95**
    Selling skills 95; Books 96; Videos 96; Audiotapes 97; Seminars and courses 97; TECs 99; Know what you are selling 99

12. **Finding a job**   **103**
    Advertisements 103; The covering letter and CV 104; The non-advertised job 106; About agencies 106; The targeted mailing 107; The interview 108; Testing, testing 109

13. **Personal security**   **111**
    Advice from the Suzy Lamplugh Trust 111

Backword   *117*

Index   *119*

Foreword

Many women in business today still suffer from a lack of equality in attitude. Too often, they receive shabby treatment from their male colleagues. Breaking out of the second-class-citizen mould is tough but not impossible!

A career in sales might be the solution. Some of the world's most successful career women are salespeople.

You may be recently out of school, or university, looking for your first real job, or a woman whose children no longer require full-time attention, or simply a long-suffering secretary ready to break out of the box.

How do you, as a woman contemplating a career in sales, start? How do you become a success? ...A person people point out as an example, a role model, for others to follow?

This book will show you. Through a series of interviews with some of the most successful women in business today, and some who are still on their way up, you will explore the challenges, the frustrations, the strategies and joys of a career as a sales leader. And you will get powerful advice from people who are there, on the firing line, working at it, right now. Helpful hints, dos and don'ts, checklists, action plans and ideas are all included. The book is aimed at women, but men are hereby given permission to read it and benefit from it.

So begin your investigation into your future career in sales right here.

Chapter 1

Why choose selling as a career?

The idea of selling as a career has often been tainted with a negative aura in the United Kingdom, whereas in many other countries salespeople are more highly regarded. Why is this so? Could it be that successful salespeople tend to make a lot of money? That they tend to be a bit forward and self-confident? That they readily display the traits of ambition? That they have a winning mentality?

These are not the commonest behaviour patterns to be found or accepted in Britain, even today.

It's a well-known fact that many British people deprecate success, especially if high earnings are involved. It is as if they were embarrassed by it. As soon as a person starts to make it in business, the newspapers can't wait to find some reason to bring them back down to the level of the great mass of grin-and-bear-it, stiff-upper-lip, muddle-through, comfortably shabby, *status quo* acceptors who make up the largest part of the population. The only people who are entitled to make a lot of money without criticism are rock musicians and sports stars. Any high earnings by successful businesspeople are reported on begrudgingly in the tabloids, along with great lists of assets, all with price tags attached, as part of the papers' drive to increase the envy level among their readers.

Breaking out of the box

Surely there are many people who want to break out of the box of mediocrity described above. These are the people who want to live in a world where extraordinary effort and success are well rewarded, where ambition can be addressed and encouraged, where a large part of the thrill and passion of life comes from making things happen. They want to live in a meritocracy, not a mediocracy! They want to be... **a success!**

Such success is available through a career in sales. This book is about making it in sales but it is not a selling skills book — there are plenty of those. It is a strategic career guide.

Advantages of a sales career

A winning career in sales offers tremendous potential, not only in earnings but also in status within your organisation. In many companies a successful sales career is a proven fast-track to senior levels.

Measurement is by results that defy argument even from the most biased critics. A successful saleswoman can become a true star within an organisation. Here's a real-life example.

Tina Tietjen, Managing Director, Video Arts Ltd

I studied physiology and biochemistry at Southampton University. I wanted to be a forensic scientist, but I failed my exams and got kicked out. I soon went hunting for a 'proper job' and I worked as a waitress, and sold socks at Marks and Spencer's in the meantime. Marks offered me a management trainee job (I was 19) but I failed the medical — something to do with wonky kneecaps. At about the same time, *The Times* newspaper was looking for classified advertising telesales people. Their ad specified age 25+. I was distinctly 25−. I wrote to them and said they absolutely must interview me before hiring anyone, and they did, and they hired me. A little bit of downright cheek can work wonders!

The Times was a wonderful place to start. They had recently become part of the Thomson organisation, which was well known for its excellent training. I struggled through my first few months in this new world of telephone sales. It was great practice. My advice to anyone starting out is to aim for an organisation that trains and develops people. *The Times* was absolutely wonderful for me — I've benefited from that start ever since.

Over the next two years I was put in charge of telesales and I had a staff of 55 people. I was then 21. I left at 23, since it was clear to me that my career development would be stunted, being young and female. I spent some time looking for my next job, and had great difficulty. I was regarded as a curiosity by those companies that chose to interview me. Not only was I young and female, but I was making a lot of money. They would tell me to my face that the reason they interviewed me was because they wanted to see what I was like, but they could never hire me because I was a woman. My attitude was simply that I wouldn't want to work for an organisation with those values anyway, so there!

I finally got a job with The Industrial Society, a major training organisation, as an adviser and trainer. I was there for eight years, ending up as a division director.

I had been doing some consultancy work with Video Arts through The Industrial Society and I joined Video Arts to do all their support materials, writing and designing these, with lots of project work. I then became head of customer services, which included sales, marketing and distribution, and eventually was named managing director of the Video Arts distribution company, while my colleague, Maggie Tree, headed the production company. We were soon both on the board of Video Arts, and when John Cleese and his partners decided to sell their interests, Maggie and I bought the business.

No experience required

Another big advantage of a sales career is that, provided you have the right sort of personality and attitude, it is quite possible to get a selling job even if you have no sales experience. If you look at a selection of entry-level advertisements for sales people, you'll see phrases like these:

- You don't need sales experience, but you must be determined and enthusiastic, with an outgoing personality. Our comprehensive training will provide you with detailed knowledge of our products and professional selling techniques (life-insurance sales).
- We require articulate and numerate sales personnel, educated to a minimum of A-level standard, preferably graduates, across the UK. You will display determination, commitment

- and have presence to communicate at the highest levels (business communications products).
- Sales experience is not a prerequisite as training is given, but we will only consider applicants who can show an exceptional educational or career path to date or outstanding flair in their own field. As we will recruit someone of above average ability, a good education, possibly to degree level (certainly 'A' level) is essential, together with a striking appearance and extrovert personality (new/used car sales).
- Lack of formal qualifications will not be a disadvantage, but the ability to demonstrate common sense is crucial (home furnishings sales).
- Articulate...Business/sales background...Foreign language speaker... Age 22–35... Earn £60K pa goal... If these are your personal qualities and ambitions then you almost certainly have what it takes to succeed in a sales career with our company (advertising telesales).

The secretarial start-up

A large number of women we interviewed for this book started out as secretaries. Being a secretary in an organisation is a good way of knowing the company. Many secretaries find themselves practically running the place, so it's not surprising that they find the move to a responsible sales position relatively easy (although, not necessarily easy to achieve). Look at what happened to this woman, who had no real sales experience.

Audrey Chessell, Senior Sales Executive, Austrian Airlines

My first job was as a secretary with Air India in London. I worked there for eight years, doing all kinds of jobs associated with working in the local base of an international airline, but I was always identified as a secretary. For example, I worked out interline arrangements — promoting sales between the airline and other airlines. If an airline had issued a ticket for a multi-leg trip, involving several

WHY CHOOSE SELLING AS A CAREER?

carriers, we wanted them to assign the appropriate legs to us rather than to a competitor, which generated a share of the fare for us. After four years I became secretary to the regional manager.

I then moved on, once again as a 'secretary', to Eastern Airlines, which was planning a Miami – London route, although at that time it did not serve London at all. After several years there doing many sales functions under the secretarial title, I went to Ethiopian Airlines as secretary to the top man, and, as before, I dealt with all aspects of the business.

Then I moved on to what was then my best job yet, with Iran Air (this was while the Shah was still around). When I started with them they were running just five 707s a week between Teheran and London, and in just over three years this grew to 34 747 flights between Teheran, London, New York and Tokyo. We had a lot of cargo and charter business, too. I was really able to make things happen here. I was the assistant to the area manager for Europe. I was always dealing with VIPs, working on promotions and dealing with our advertising agencies. Then came the revolution, the service dropped to one 707 a week, and I left.

Next stop was Western Airlines, where I was called an agency and interline executive. My job was to develop the forthcoming London – Honolulu route, via Anchorage. However, the airline went out of business before the route started, so I moved on to a temporary assignment with Icelandair. It was supposed to last two weeks and ended up at eleven months. I was the acting deputy station manager, once again a Jill of all trades.

Finally I joined Austrian Airlines, where I work now. Guess what I was hired as? A secretary! But after a year, they actually called me a sales executive. And that's what I am today. My principal task is to sell Austria as a venue for conferences and meetings, especially the incentive travel market (where people at a company get the trip as a reward for sales performance, for example). We have tremendous hotel and meeting facilities in Vienna, and now, particularly with the opening up of eastern Europe, we're very conveniently located. I'm paid a straight salary, and of course there are the attractive travel perks that come from working for an airline.

> The most valuable tool I have is the ability to network. I belong to lots of associations and clubs and I am always at some function, often as a guest speaker. People know they can call on me for advice.

In my own case, my first job was as a secretary to a group of account executives (sales people), at Merrill Lynch, in Boston. After a while, I thought it would be nice to work on the trading desk, which was a sales function. It never occurred to me to ask for such a change at Merrill. I went to a competitor, Smith Barney, and applied for a trainee job, which they gave me, based on the fact that I was at Merrill. Then I went in to my boss to resign, and he asked me why I hadn't asked for such a job at Merrill. 'I simply didn't think of it,' I said. 'I guess I thought it would be offered to me.'

'Don't assume anything,' he said, 'If you want something, ask for it! We are not mind readers!' That's good advice. If you want something, ask for it! If you assume, it makes an **ass** out of **u** and **me!**

Women in sales

Successful selling is about listening to people, about satisfying their needs or expectations. Women are typically good listeners.

Women who have experience in raising a family bring an extra dimension to the sales job. Because they have had to attend to the needs of a variety of people in a family role, they have accumulated an excellent background. Personally I found the task of selling much easier when I returned to the role after bringing up my two children to school age. Before I had my family, when I was in my early twenties, I lacked confidence and experience. Yes, I had taken confidence-building courses and selling-skills programmes galore, but nothing served me like the experience of bringing up two small children. And let's face it, most customers tend to behave like small children!

Women *vs* men

When I joined the final month of the Merrill Lynch training programme in New York in 1975, I was one of three women in a class of 85! These days, there are far more women working in a selling role. But the business world is still dominated by men, especially in my area (big-ticket asset-based finance). In four years of working in this area of business in the UK, I have found myself selling to a woman decision-maker precisely once! There are, however, often women in support roles when I sell, such as lawyers, accountants, administrative people and the like. They are part of my audience.

I believe that being a woman in this business is neither an advantage nor a disadvantage. I have no preference as to whether I deal with a man or a woman when I sell. Other women have other opinions, however. Some love to sell to women; others much prefer selling to men, or even hate dealing with women customers.

There's no question that, when the sales audience is mostly young men, the strategy of fielding a team of attractive young women as salespeople has been found to be very effective.

As far as harassment is concerned, it goes with the territory. I find the higher the level I'm selling to, the less harassment there is. Actually, there is very little from customers. But from fellow salesmen, that's a different story! Imagine what it must have been like in New York, one of three women among over 80 men! In 1975, the acceptance of women in sales was still a bit of a struggle, even in the United States. Fifteen years later, at Atlantic Computers, the salesmen still tried to keep up to their self-image of unquestionable attractiveness. A firm businesslike response always put them in their place, I found.

Most of the men/women problems have to do with the attitudes of the men. But these days, it's getting to be history. It's been a process of evolution.

Patricia Leach, Director Franchise Operations, Frost & Sullivan

When I was at grammar school, I was told the only jobs for women were teaching, nursing or banking. None of these interested me. So at the age of 19 I started a retail boutique in south-east London. I began by selling children's wear, mostly baby clothes. The business grew up with my customers and it wasn't long before I was selling clothes for older children.

After a few years, I joined Marks & Spencer as a management trainee. This was a very tough regime, and not really my cup of tea, so I left after six months. I joined Collins Publishing as an educational sales representative selling textbooks to schools. Since I had a young family, this was convenient. I needed an interesting position that would fit in with family life and here I worked during school hours and term time only. I was paid a straight salary. Collins welcomed women in this role.

I worked at Collins for six years, ending up in head office working in their export sales business. This was more of a management job, with other salespeople doing the travelling. I felt that in this role I was held back because of being a woman — they did not want women to do any travelling.

I joined Frost & Sullivan about eight years ago. This is an international company, with several offices in Europe, and so I started to travel on sales trips. We have two main operations. We run seminars for business and we do market studies about different industries, which we sell. I concentrate in the seminar area. Some of the seminars are open to the public, others are especially produced for the client. We do about 500 seminars a year. We are in the process of franchising the seminars abroad, for example in southern Europe, the Far East and Indonesia, and we're now expanding to the Middle East. They are mostly about information technology or various management issues.

I was hired originally as a seminar sales representative — I saw the ad in the newspaper. I'm paid a salary and commission. When I joined, most of our seminars were for the public. I started developing corporate clients, with the idea of putting on private seminars for their own people, and a growing part of our business is done that way now.

I have several sales people working for me now. What do I look for when I'm hiring? I want people I can get along with personally. We're leaning to relationship managers, lined up with specific industries, so good personal communication skills are essential, as well as experience within the industry. I look for a vibrant personality. They have to know how to create trust by showing a genuine interest in the client and caring that the results are right.

I look for a positive attitude, a person who does not like to fail, one who is tenacious and cares enough to attend to the smallest detail. That's the bottom line.

Let's take a closer look at what it takes to make it in sales.

Chapter 2
Know thyself

Selling requires many different personalities — companies with large sales forces often look for people from different backgrounds and with different styles and personality traits. Some people are good prospectors, researching, identifying and contacting new business opportunities and setting the stage. Others are good presenters, excelling at the appetising and succinct explanation of the features and benefits of the product or service. Then there are the closers — the ones who get the customer to sign on the dotted line. These people are skilled at overcoming objections and negotiating the fine points that can make the difference between deal and no deal. And the very best enjoy these traits in combination.

Is selling for you? You need to have a good idea of what motivates you to answer that question. You can rest assured that many sales jobs involve a fairly thorough set of aptitude tests, so it is not likely that you will be hired unless you have 'the right stuff'. To get a feel for these tests and to help you evaluate yourself, try a book called *Test Your Own Aptitude* by J Barrett and G Williams, published by Kogan Page. But take a quick look at yourself right now so you can get a good feeling about your prospects as a salesperson, or stop wasting your time.

According to Ann Isaacs, head of the London career counselling firm Executive Action, there are several key attributes a person should have to be successful in a sales career. How do you measure up in these areas? Rate yourself with the checklist below.

Positive traits evaluation chart

Attribute	High				Low
Lively personality	☐	☐	☐	☐	☐
A sense of self-confidence	☐	☐	☐	☐	☐

MAKING IT IN SALES

Attribute	High				Low
Willingness to take a risk	☐	☐	☐	☐	☐
Willingness to fail	☐	☐	☐	☐	☐
Willingness to appraise self	☐	☐	☐	☐	☐
Willingness to learn	☐	☐	☐	☐	☐
Persuasiveness	☐	☐	☐	☐	☐
Perseverance	☐	☐	☐	☐	☐
Likes dealing with people	☐	☐	☐	☐	☐
Likes to win	☐	☐	☐	☐	☐
Success oriented	☐	☐	☐	☐	☐
High energy level	☐	☐	☐	☐	☐
A sense of humour/fun	☐	☐	☐	☐	☐
Witty	☐	☐	☐	☐	☐
Imaginative	☐	☐	☐	☐	☐
Creative	☐	☐	☐	☐	☐
Good communication skills	☐	☐	☐	☐	☐
Good listener	☐	☐	☐	☐	☐
Enthusiastic	☐	☐	☐	☐	☐
Understands it is a win/lose game	☐	☐	☐	☐	☐
Able to handle rejection	☐	☐	☐	☐	☐
Self-starter	☐	☐	☐	☐	☐

In contrast, below are the personality traits of a person who is not suited to a career in sales. Could this really be you? If so, try something else!

Negative traits evaluation chart

Attribute	High				Low
Uncompetitive	☐	☐	☐	☐	☐
Prefers dealing with things *vs* people	☐	☐	☐	☐	☐
Doesn't like to be measured	☐	☐	☐	☐	☐
Likes a safe job and quiet life	☐	☐	☐	☐	☐
Doesn't want surprises	☐	☐	☐	☐	☐

KNOW THYSELF

Attribute	High				Low
Tends towards pessimism	☐	☐	☐	☐	☐
Tends to follow the crowd	☐	☐	☐	☐	☐
Wants everything cut and dried	☐	☐	☐	☐	☐

Just to be absolutely sure, here are some more characteristics. Go through this list and rate your capabilities in these areas:

More positives

Attribute	High				Low
I have no problem walking up to a perfect stranger and asking for directions.	☐	☐	☐	☐	☐
If I have to explain complicated travel directions myself, I can do this clearly and people have no problem following them.	☐	☐	☐	☐	☐
I'd like to make a lot more money than I do right now.	☐	☐	☐	☐	☐
I enjoy writing letters about projects in which I am involved.	☐	☐	☐	☐	☐
I love to learn. I'm always willing to experience new ideas.	☐	☐	☐	☐	☐
I enjoy interacting with people, finding out their interests and developing a level of communication.	☐	☐	☐	☐	☐
If I have received bad service in a restaurant, I make a point of telling them about it.	☐	☐	☐	☐	☐
I get very motivated when I'm given a seemingly impossible challenge and a very tight deadline.	☐	☐	☐	☐	☐

Attribute	High				Low
If I see a colleague pulling ahead of me on a similar assignment, I redouble my efforts.	☐	☐	☐	☐	☐
I enjoy talking on the telephone.	☐	☐	☐	☐	☐
I have a wide variety of interests and can converse on many different subjects.	☐	☐	☐	☐	☐

If you score mostly in the two left boxes, get on with your sales career! Just to reinforce the concept, how do you rate in these areas?

More ratings

Attribute	High				Low
I am very content with the way I live now. I see no point in busting myself to make a bit more money.	☐	☐	☐	☐	☐
I am easily intimidated.	☐	☐	☐	☐	☐
I don't read a lot.	☐	☐	☐	☐	☐
I hate computers and modern gadgetry.	☐	☐	☐	☐	☐
When I am explaining something to someone, I usually have to go through it three or four times before they get it.	☐	☐	☐	☐	☐
I have trouble expressing myself on paper.	☐	☐	☐	☐	☐
I would prefer not to have to get up and make a speech to a crowd of strangers.	☐	☐	☐	☐	☐
I like to be told what to do when I work.	☐	☐	☐	☐	☐

KNOW THYSELF

Attribute	High				Low
If I have ordered a meal and the delivery is not exactly what I wanted, I pretend nothing is wrong.	☐	☐	☐	☐	☐

By now, you should have a good idea whether to continue reading this book!

Let's assume you feel right about a selling career, and if you're this far into the book, I guess you do. What types of selling should you aim for? There are two ways of looking at this question:

- What do you want to sell?
- To whom/how do you want to sell it?

Let's look at these in more detail, and use some worksheets to come up with our answers.

What do you want to sell?

The best thing for you to sell is something you're really interested in. That way you can work long hours and still love it!

If skiing is your life, you could sell skiing equipment in a retail outlet, or wholesale for the manufacturer or distributor, or you could sell advertising space for a ski magazine, or you could sell ski holidays for a travel company.

If rock music is your love, you could sell recorded music at retail, or you could sell musical instruments, or work for a music school, or a recording studio, or a record company, or a talent agency. Here's a real-life example of a woman who turned her interest into a sales career.

Lisa Barnwell, Sales Manager, Café Royal

I've always been interested in the hotel and catering business. My father works for British Airways, so I travelled all over the world, staying in lots of hotels, as I grew up. Hence, part of my education was to get a national diploma in hotel, catering and institutional operations. After this, my first job was with a small hotel near London as a management trainee, where I worked for a year. Then I went to the Compleat Angler Hotel in Marlow, where I worked as a front-desk receptionist. This is where I started my selling experience, getting involved in developing functions at the hotel.

After a year there, I spent a year at London's Royal Horse Guards Hotel, working in sales, honing my skills. I took a lot of internal sales-training courses there. Then I went to Resotel, a global hotel reservations service. I spent two years there as a senior sales executive. I had a car and was paid a straight salary. My job was to call on organisations throughout south-east England, developing new business for our reservations service with companies and organisations in the area. We undertook to provide reservations at hotels throughout the world, so my targets were firms with people who did a lot of worldwide travelling.

I've been with the Café Royal for just a few months. My job is to offer our services as a venue for meetings, conferences and events, such as receptions and dinners. We have eight floors of facilities with conference and banqueting space. We can handle up to 1000 guests in our Empire Napoleon Room, so you can see we have a lot of scope for different activities.

My customers are large organisations, mostly in the London and south-east UK areas. I spend a lot of time meeting with executives of these entities, helping them plan their event. A nice part of my job is that I see it right through, actually being there on the night. So there's a lot of satisfaction and feedback in experiencing the results of my work taking place.

I love what I do. Café Royal is quite high profile. The biggest reward is seeing a project I've put together coming through and being a big success. And the biggest frustration is spending a lot of time and energy on a project and having it all fall through due to outside circumstances. But you have to learn not to take this kind of thing personally. A positive attitude keeps you going and brings you on to greater success in the future.

Area of interest or hobby 👉 Area of activity	1	2	3
Who retails this?			
Who makes this?			
Who wholesales or distributes this?			
What publications cover this?			
In what other ways could I be involved in this area in a sales capacity?			
Any other ideas?			
What else?			

Making a choice

Here's a way to check out the situation for yourself. Using the table above, write down three things or hobbies you are really interested in as the headings for columns 1, 2 and 3. Then look at the areas of activity listed in the left-hand column and write in answers for each area of interest. For example, if your interest is bicycling, you might write Halfords or Toys R Us in the retailing box, Raleigh in the 'Who makes this?' box, and so on. Fill in as many answers as possible. Don't settle for just one per box.

Soon you will have a matrix of appropriate targets for you to consider in your career development.

But before you go too far down that line, you need to consider *how* you might be involved in selling. This has a lot to do with *to whom* you would like to sell.

To whom/how do you want to sell?

Now we get into the way you will work. Selling can involve lots of ancillary activities or considerations, such as:

- Identifying and researching prospective customers
- Cold calling by telephone
- Writing prospecting letters
- Cold calling in person
- Responding to advertising leads
- Visiting the customer
- Making a presentation, one-to-one
- Making a presentation to a group of people
- Extensive travel
- Working from an office
- Working from home
- Staying in one location
- Attending trade shows
- Entertaining customers
- Immediate transaction time
- Short transaction time
- Medium transaction time
- Long transaction time
- Low price, low commission
- Medium price, medium commission
- High price, high commission

In the next chapters, we'll look at the different types of selling jobs, what they involve and how they compare.

Chapter 3
What is selling? Understanding the opportunities

There are selling jobs and there are jobs where you have to sell. What does this mean? Let's look at the distinctions.

Types of selling

Many selling jobs have the word 'sales' in the job title — sales representative, sales executive, sales consultant, those kinds of things. The task in such jobs is pretty cut and dried. Here is the product or service. These are the customers or potential buyers. Sell it! When you do, you'll earn a piece of the action in the form of a sales commission.

Then there are the jobs that don't use the word 'sales' in their titles — account executive, financial counsellor, adviser, consultant, marketing executive, and such like. In these types of job, selling is often an important and essential component, but it may be incidental to the overall activity. What is sold may be ideas rather than a specific commodity. It may be that no money changes hands as a result of the sale, and that there is no commission earned from the successful outcome. But it is selling, nonetheless. Here's a real-life example.

> **Cathy Rowan, independent consultant, Career & Organisational Development**
>
> I've been an independent consultant in my field, career counselling, for about a year now. I expect to be going into partnership with a colleague soon, to offer a broader service. Right now I'm working on a three-month contract with a major outplacement firm.
>
> Before going on my own, I worked with KPMG Peat Marwick for five years. I was hired as an executive selection and search consultant.

My clients were senior management people in large organisations. About half the positions I was seeking to fill were financial directors and the like. The rest were other senior managers. My job involved, at first, dealing with the client — the organisation wanting to hire someone. I would take their brief on the kind of person they needed, helping them to define the specifications, and then I would write a proposal, which would lead to writing the advertisement, working with the client until we agreed on final copy. Then I would place the ad through our advertising agency, perhaps getting involved in selecting which publications to use (although they were usually *The Sunday Times* and *The Financial Times*).

I would then deal with the responses to the ad, screening them down to a short list. I would conduct the preliminary interviews and make recommendations to the client. Hence this job involved a sort of three-way selling mode. First I was selling KPMG to the client. Then I was selling the client to the candidate. And I was selling the candidate to the client.

After 18 months in this role, I transferred to the career counselling area, basically advising and working with people who had been made redundant. This is the area I specialise in today.

Before KPMG, I was with ICL, the computer company, in the head-office personnel department, and for five years before that I was with Chloride Group in the same field.

I started my career in sales. After graduating from Reading University, I joined British Airways as a telephone sales representative — basically doing reservations work. I wanted to do this for a year, while I took stock of my career prospects. This was an excellent starting point for me, because we got good training and the telephone work with all kinds of people taught me a lot about presenting myself and the company. I did this for a year, and then decided I wanted to get into personnel work, so I took a full-time course in personnel management for a year.

For independent consultants, sales is a major part of the job. In fact, if that's your role, realise you must always be in 'sales' mode, but in a low-key way. There's nobody else to represent you. As an independent, it's not enough to be good at your job. There are probably plenty of people who are good at what you do. You have to go beyond that. It's essential that the initial impression you create and your presentation always be A1, so that those aspects layer on top of the work you do. And this philosophy applies with all your contacts, because you never know whom you're going to meet from day to day. You can't have an 'off' day. There's nowhere to hide.

The people you meet are always part of your network base, and, in turn, you are part of their network. The progress you make is the result of the impact you make and whom you know. So become an expert at networking, and keep at it!

Selling in spite of the title

As another example, take an account executive in a public relations agency who is responsible for serving the communications needs of the client — organising a press conference, writing a press release, placing a story, setting up an interview. Where does the selling come in? In several ways:

- Selling the firm to the client in the first place
- Selling the firm's ideas to the client
- Selling a story to a publication
- Selling an interview to a TV show
- Looking for opportunities for more business

Imagine you are a management consultant, like Cathy, above. Your task is to give advice and counselling on, let's say, quality programmes in manufacturing. Does not that role include:

- Selling the firm to the client in the first place?
- Selling the firm's ideas to the client?
- Looking for opportunities for more business?

Truly, there are selling activities required. And the same goes for many other relationship jobs.

However, let's concentrate on the straight sales jobs for now.

Ways of selling

There are many ways of selling, for example:
- Retail sales in a shop or other location
- Door-to-door sales
- Houseparty selling
- Telephone sales (proactive — calling to generate business; and reactive — answering the phone and taking orders)
- Sales where the customer comes to you
- Sales where you go to the customer
- Sales where demonstrations are needed
- Sales requiring technical support
- Sales where you need technical expertise
- Sales where you need minimum qualifications or certification

and many more.

In fact, you can group all these ways into five major categories:

- Direct sales
- Multi-level marketing (network sales)
- Retail sales
- Telephone sales
- Business-to-business sales

In the next five chapters, we take these five core types of selling activity and break them down into more detail as to:

- Typical areas of business in which they are found
- Qualifications required
- Customers
- Tasks
- Lifestyle
- Attributes required
- Typical transaction times
- The typical advertisement for the job

Then we invite you to list whom you know in each area to talk to about it. Talking to someone who is already doing the job is a very good way of finding out if that role is for you.

Finally, to give you a flavour of the real world, we relate some true experiences provided by one or two women working in each field right now. If you make use of this analytical review, you should be able to decide what types of selling interest you.

Let's start with direct sales.

Chapter 4
Direct sales

Selling directly to the customer, probably in their home or office, is really the toughest area of sales. Because very few qualifications are required, direct selling attracts a lot of people who have trouble finding other employment, but the vast majority of them will never make it. Since it is a tough game, personnel turnover is high and the whole area has a relatively poor image. However, if you are good — really good, and can distinguish yourself, you can do very well in direct sales.

There's a whole additional aspect of direct sales, called multi-level marketing or network sales. This is covered separately in the next chapter.

To get a feel for the tougher aspects of the direct sales business, I recommend three excellent films: *The Tin Men* (starring Richard Dreyfus and Danny de Vito, about aluminium-siding salesmen in Baltimore); *Glengarry, Glen Ross* (starring Jack Lemmon and Alan Arkin, about real estate salesmen in Florida) and *Paper Moon* (starring Ryan and Tatum O'Neal, about a 1930's bible salesman in the US midwest).

Typical areas

- Life insurance
- Other financial services (eg, pensions, annuities, savings plans, etc)
- Residential property
- Timesharing property
- Home improvements (eg, double glazing, kitchens, bathrooms, driveways, environmental equipment)
- Household goods (eg, brushes, soaps, etc)
- Cosmetics
- Jewellery
- Apparel (especially lingerie)

Qualifications

- Usually nothing more than a 'sales personality', although some qualifications are required in the financial services area, dealt with by training programmes usually supplied by the company.

Customers

- Individuals of all types — almost anybody
- People who work in businesses

Tasks

- Identifying, researching and qualifying prospective customers
- Cold calling by telephone (lots)
- Writing prospecting letters (lots)
- Cold calling in person (lots)
- Responding to advertising leads
- Getting referrals
- Visiting the prospect/customer
- Door-to-door sales (some areas)
- Houseparty selling (some areas)
- Making a presentation, one-to-one
- Making a presentation to a group of people

Compensation

- Mostly straight commission, sometimes with a draw (advance) against future earnings
- High rewards if successful; low to zero rewards if not

Lifestyle

- Hard work

DIRECT SALES

- Long hours
- Plenty of local travel to customers' locations; car important
- Plenty of rejection
- Usually operating from home, perhaps with visits to a local sales office

Attributes required

- Self-starter
- Self-confidence
- Positive mental attitude
- Resilience
- Ambition
- Sense of humour
- Flexibility
- Persuasiveness
- Perseverance
- Likes dealing with people
- High energy level

Transaction time

- Immediate (low-price, low-return areas)
- Short to medium (high-price, high-return areas)

Whom do you know to talk to about direct selling?

_____
_____
_____
_____
_____
_____

Sample direct sales job advertisement

We believe in success but not at any price.

In the sense that profit is the lifeblood of business, financial services is no different from any other industry. However, if you're unfamiliar with our world, you'd be forgiven for thinking that everyone in it worships at the altar of money. Of course, some do, but then there will always be those who are motivated solely by short-term financial gain.

(Company name) is a very different kind of business looking for a very different kind of sales person. For a start, we believe in building long-term client relationships, based on integrity, commitment to service and mutual trust. All qualities, in fact, that money can't buy.

We're anxious not to waste your time or make promises that can't be fulfilled. Three interviews will tell us about your strengths and we will do our best to make sure you know about us. We only take on those people with a genuine chance of succeeding in a competitive market. So, once chosen, you can feel confident of having all the qualities needed to achieve real rewards. To that end, maximum earnings are unlimited and to show our commitment we will provide a guaranteed level of financial support.

As part of (Parent Company), our training will do the rest. Twice a week, for two years, you will receive all the tuition and professional advice that you need, with constant encouragement to fulfil your potential. While from day one, your guaranteed financial package will give you a solid start as you build your customer relationships.

We feel it's a unique offer, but one worth making to attract mature, confident, business-like people. If that sounds like you, please find out more — contact the manager at your nearest branch, or write to...

Real-life experience

Betina Birtchnell, Financial Consultant, Helm Financial Services Ltd

I sell life insurance and pension-type investments. Last year I made about £70 000, and this year I'll top £100 000. I started about eight years ago, joining Abbey Life as a trainee. I am a Dane, and I moved to England in 1969, working in the travel industry, after training as a bookkeeper in Denmark. I also worked for the Danish Embassy in London in the visa section for several years. I moved over to the insurance business because I wanted a change and I like a challenge. Also, having a family, I believe in the importance of financial security.

I joined Abbey Life, going through their extensive training programme. After about five weeks at my local branch, I attended the Abbey Life training school for a week, learning the rudiments about a couple of basic products. During this training period, there was no salary at all. They pay straight commission. Within a couple of months of graduation I had already doubled my embassy salary, and things continued to improve thereafter.

This business is tough. Ninety-five per cent of the people who enter the field are not in it a year later. It takes a lot of cold calling to develop business. I did not like doing this by phone — I tend to see things in black and white, and you need a more flexible approach on the phone. Another thing I didn't like about the phone was that you don't really know who you are going to see, so there is a security aspect there. So I started cold calling by knocking on doors. During the week I would call on shopkeepers and small businesses near where I live. On Saturdays, I would call on private homes. Typically, 100 calls would result in five appointments, which in turn would result in two sales. As I got more experienced, I'd set up more appointments per 100 and turn more of these into sales. I always found it better to meet the people personally to set up the appointment. You never expect to sell on the first meeting, of course.

I left Abbey for Helm after two and a half years. Helm is an independent broker, so my positioning is now that of a consultant advising on financial planning needs rather than a salesperson with a quota to meet. I'm treated more as a professional now, more like a solicitor or accountant. My clients often introduce me to their friends. I don't overtly ask for referrals, but I get them.

I love this business. One day I'm in a boardroom, the next I'm in a council house. One day I'm dealing with someone making £200 000 a year, the next someone on £10 000. I can dress up or down, depending on who I'm seeing that day. Being a Dane, I don't have any of this typical British class problem. People from all walks of life accept me without any hidden barriers. It's always interesting and challenging. I don't know how else I could make this kind of income these days.

What does this business take? Discipline, hard work, determination, patience, perseverance, it's really quite obvious. Life insurance is probably the most difficult thing to sell. If you can sell this, you can sell anything!

Elizabeth Ayles, Branch Manager, Howard Cundey & Company, Estate Agents

I came into sales through the secretarial route. My parents insisted that I go to secretarial college when I left school and my first job after that was as a secretary to a firm of architects and land agents. Thus I entered the property field, in an indirect way, right from the start.

However, over the next four or five years, I stayed as a secretary, holding various jobs, in East Grinstead, London and Birmingham, and during this time I got married. In 1975, we moved back to East Grinstead, and I had a choice of two jobs. I chose the lower-paid one because it seemed more interesting.

It was with Taylor & Tester, estate agents and auctioneers, as secretary to the manager. I just had the feeling it would offer me a better career opportunity. I was right. Working in this capacity, I really found out all about the business, and the breakthrough came one day (after a couple of years) when my boss asked me to prepare a property for auction. This meant developing all the specifications, writing the descriptions and producing all the documentation. It was the first time in their organisation that a woman had been involved in this process. Pretty soon, I was doing this a lot, although I was still called, and paid as, a secretary.

After a while I became a negotiator, which means I would help people who were looking for a property to identify candidates, and I would help people looking to sell to prepare their properties for market. This included visiting the site, taking the measurements, preparing the description and producing the prospectus.

The primary requirement in this job is very good 'people' skills — being able to talk to a variety of people from all walks of life about something very basic and close to home, as it were. You have to be a really good listener and judge of character so you can translate an often inarticulate description of needs into a property solution. You have to know the right sorts of questions to ask to draw out their real needs, which have a lot to do with lifestyle and ambiance, so you can show the right kinds of listings to the prospect.

We were mostly involved in fairly large country properties with a lot of land. I was paid a very good basic salary, plus a very small commission. By the time I left to have my first child, in 1979, I was a senior negotiator.

Two children later, I re-entered the employment world in 1987. I was rehired by my old firm on a part-time basis, to help them on Saturdays. My job was very lowly. I was literally doing the filing and the photocopying. For some reason, I found myself very nervous about being back at work. I had somehow lost a lot of confidence staying at home. It took me about three months to get it back, which happened when I discovered I was actually being effective in what I was doing. There was no thought of any training — everything was learned 'on the job'.

The following year, the company was bought out by a large building society. I was made a full-time negotiator and soon I was asked to be the training officer for the division — the advantage of big-company thinking. This involved going up north for training seminars and meeting people from all over the country, and then giving training in my area, which was a tremendous experience.

A year later, I was given the job of manager of our local office, but I was told that since this was quite a big jump for me, I would not immediately be paid as such — a perfect way to make me feel good! Whereas all the male negotiators and managers had company cars, it was not thought appropriate to give me one. However, a few months later, one of the men was sacked, and they said: 'You don't really want his old car, do you?' Of course, I said yes, so I finally got a company car, albeit not a new one. This was in 1989, at the height of the property boom. I did pretty well. But then things started to top out. At the end of 1990, I got a new boss, a woman. I thought this would be great, but I was wrong. In fact it was terrible. She told me I was useless and couldn't manage anything if I tried. The company's preference was to hire young men, barely out of their teens and pay them a pittance.

Things got so bad, I was offered the opportunity to be retrained as a junior secretary. I left. Almost immediately I was hired by my present company to manage one of their four offices. I've been there 18 months, and although these times are tough in the property world, we are making it. In our business, the only income comes from selling properties, so it focuses the mind. You have to recognise every opportunity. You have to understand houses are not sold, they are bought. It's the way a person feels about a property that will make it happen. That's why I say you need to be a good judge of character. The task is simply to get a clear mental image of the sort of house this person, or family, would like, and then show them the ones you've got that fit that type of specification. It's a form of matchmaking. You really need to like people.

I recently hired a negotiator. I was looking for a certain type of person, and I had every candidate telephone me initially. I can judge a person a lot from how they are on the phone. The woman I hired was 23, with no experience. But she had absolutely the right personality, a nice voice and she came over perfectly — friendly and relaxed.

Being relaxed is important, especially in these tough times. Ninety-nine per cent of the people who come in to see us are unhappy. They're having money problems or marriage problems or both, and buying or selling a house is a very stressful situation for them. It may be something they *have* to do rather than want to do. So they walk in the door with their aggressiveness already powered up. Hence it's essential to be thick skinned and quietly assertive in dealing with them. Once they've exchanged contracts, they become nice people again.

It's still the case that there are no qualifications or licence required to be a property negotiator, but the government is starting to clamp down on the way things are represented by salespeople, and I don't think it will be long before requirements get a bit more formal, with training and exams being needed. That's the way it is in a lot of other countries. And about time too!

Chapter 5
Multi-level marketing (network marketing)

Many people, especially those involved in it, say that network marketing is the wave of the future. We'll let you be the judge. To get an overview on the business, it's best to ask an expert. That's Peter Clothier, a former Trading Standards Officer and author of the Kogan Page book *Multi-Level Marketing — A practical guide to successful network selling*, which was one of the top three best-selling business books in the UK in 1991.

The following is an article on MLM from this book. It is copyright © 1992 Peter Clothier, and is reprinted here with permission.

Often the subject of enquiries by members of the public to Trading Standards Departments, multi-level marketing (MLM) has for too long been shrouded in mystery and misunderstanding. In this article I will attempt to give you the facts about this successful, legal and increasingly popular method of doing business.

What is multi-level marketing?

Also known as network marketing, MLM is a rapidly expanding method of selling goods and services which is now firmly established in most countries of the free world. It is big business, probably offering the opportunity for wealth to more people than any other form of business. Worldwide sales through MLM are over ten billion dollars annually and thousands of people have reached millionaire status by taking advantage of the concept.

The basic principle of MLM which makes it different from conventional business is that, instead of a manufacturer constructing a large administrative and sales organisation comprised of employees, self-employed distributors are encouraged to build a sales organisation of persons like themselves by their own efforts. Financial rewards are paid based upon total sales of all distributors within the organisation developed by any particular distributor. In such a way, distributors are paid in proportion to their efforts in selling and sponsoring others (recruiting).

The types of goods and services available through MLM cover virtually every corner of consumer spending: household necessities, slimming products, perfumes, cosmetics, books, food supplements, water filtration systems, financial services, security devices, etc, and new products are appearing at an ever-increasing rate.

The attractions of MLM include:

1. The availability of very high incomes from part-time work;
2. The lack of any significant financial or other risks;
3. The ability to start and build the business successfully without any previous experience or special skills.

Stockholding is unnecessary and products should be purchased only to fulfil orders already obtained, and for a minimum demonstration stock.

We are not talking about 'get rich quick' schemes here, although exceptional people may be able to do so. The overheads normally spent on employees, marketing and advertising in conventional businesses are available instead to pass on to distributors in commission and bonuses. The high incomes possible are due to 'residual' income, ie income based upon previous efforts. Insurance agents, writers and actors earn residual income, provided the policies continue, the books still sell and so on. So in MLM, as long as the products sell regularly and your organisation grows, then your residual income increases due to your past efforts in sponsoring. 'Linear' income, ie a month's pay for a month's work, is always limited to certain levels whereas residual income is, in theory, unlimited. However, it must be remembered that MLM is like any other business inasmuch as high rewards are solely the product of hard work.

Safeguards are built in to reputable schemes to ensure that there are no short cuts to success and that the cornerstone of the business consists of retail sales to the public. Some schemes require regular purchases by distributors for their own use, thereby increasing the business volume and therefore the profit of each distributor's group. The most stable and successful companies' schemes are firmly based upon repeat purchases of quality products by satisfied customers.

Complaints

Most justifiable complaints relating to MLM are caused by the overenthusiastic, unethical and occasionally illegal activities of distributors. Problems are usually related to:

1. Exaggerated claims about the products;
2. Misleading information given at business presentations;
3. Misleading advertising for product sales or recruits;
4. New distributors being encouraged to purchase large quantities of goods in order to obtain a higher discount or position.

Contact with the relevant promoting company will hopefully result in swift action against the problem distributor, who is probably breaching the company's rules of conduct.

Common questions about MLM

Isn't it pyramid selling? The Oxford English Dictionary defines the term as 'A form of financial trickery...'. Although the term is often used to describe MLM, it is more appropriate to reserve its use for the highly undesirable and now illegal schemes which became a public menace in the early 1970s, where participants were encouraged to purchase large consignments of goods — the larger the quantity, the bigger the discount — before ensuring that they had the customers and the additional participants to supply them to. Naturally many people were left considerably out of pocket with vast stocks of unsold product. The most objectionable aspect of the schemes was that large entry fees were extracted from new participants (for the benefit of the promoter and/or the person introducing them) by holding out the prospect of receiving similar payments from further new participants. The publicity created by these schemes prompted the government to take action by means of the Fair Trading Act 1973 which outlawed them, although there are still many borderline cases around.

Won't it saturate? Some simple mathematics can demonstrate that, if every participant brings in one new recruit each week, the number of distributors in any one scheme will be greater than the population of the UK within six months. This is fine in theory, but a nonsense when some facts are considered:

1. The oldest MLM company in the world has been steadily expanding for almost 20 years in the UK alone and its UK distributors number less than one in 1000 of the population.
2. The UK birth rate is many times higher than the rate of increase in numbers in any major MLM scheme.
3. Saturation of any particular area is unlikely due to the facility of being able to sponsor persons living anywhere in the UK (or internationally, in some cases) without undue difficulty.
4. It has never yet happened!

Is it better to get in at the start? According to many advertisements for 'groundfloor' opportunities and many people within MLM and without, the answer is yes. I do not believe that this is correct. Following on from the arguments above, there will always be a certain proportion of the population who will want to participate in any particular scheme, and because of the dynamic nature of populations, I suggest that it is no more difficult to find prospective distributors or customers at a later stage of a scheme than it is at the start. It is also true that some of the most successful distributors started their business very recently in terms of the age of the companies concerned. It is possible that a distributor may be better off dealing with a well-established, stable and financially sound company than a brand new one.

Legislation

Apart from legislation covering many aspects of specific products, Part XI of the Fair Trading Act 1973 and regulations made thereunder govern certain aspects of the operations of MLM schemes.

Virtually every MLM scheme comes within the scope of section 118 of the 1973 Act and is therefore obliged to operate within the rules set down in the Pyramid Selling Schemes Regulations 1989 and 1990 and in section 120 of the Act. These regulations supersede the 1973 regulations and are directed principally to providing full details of the scheme to any prospective distributor, including the requirement for a detailed written agreement to be signed by all participants, stating their extensive rights to refunds on goods and other materials purchased if they decide to leave the scheme at any time. Payments exceeding £75 within seven days of joining a scheme are prohibited and a statutory warning against buying excessive stock must be given.

Finally

What advice can be given to a prospective distributor who wants to know whether to join a MLM scheme? I suggest the following.

Look at some of the numerous other MLM companies besides the one you may be asked to join. Carefully compare the quality, range and price of the products and the different marketing plans and distributor rules of each company. Then ask yourself these questions:

1. Would you buy the products yourself?
2. Are you satisfied with the integrity and stability of the company?
3. Are you willing to put in a significant amount of consistent effort?

If all three answers are yes, there's a lot of money waiting for you, so get started, there's nothing to lose.

MLM companies who are members of the Direct Selling Association are subjected to a substantial and continual examination of all aspects of their business by the DSA Council to ensure a good deal for distributors and customers alike. Details of member companies, which include most of the largest MLM companies, can be obtained from the Direct Selling Association, 29 Floral Street, London WC2E 9DP.

Typical areas

- Apparel (especially lingerie)
- Books
- Cosmetics
- Diet plans and foods, nutritional supplements
- Household environmental equipment
- Household goods (eg, brushes, soaps, etc)
- Jewellery
- Videos

Qualifications

- Usually nothing more than a 'sales personality' and a willingness to work hard.

Customers

- Individuals of all types – almost anybody

Tasks

- Identifying, researching and qualifying prospective customers and new distributors
- Recruiting distributors
- Cold calling by telephone
- Writing prospecting letters
- Cold calling in person
- Responding to advertising leads
- Getting referrals
- Visiting the prospect/customer
- Door-to-door sales (some areas)
- Houseparty selling (some areas)
- Making a presentation, one-to-one
- Making a presentation to a group of people
- Motivating people in your groups

Compensation

- Straight commission on direct sales and shares in the commission of people in your network
- High to very high rewards if successful; low to zero rewards if not

Lifestyle

- Hard work
- Long hours
- Plenty of local travel to customers' locations; car important
- Plenty of rejection
- Usually operating from home
- Plenty of motivational meetings

Attributes required

- Self-starter
- Self-confidence
- Positive mental attitude
- Resilience
- Ambition
- Sense of humour
- Flexibility
- Persuasiveness
- Perseverance
- Likes dealing with people
- High energy level
- Motivator

Transaction time

- Immediate to short-term

MAKING IT IN SALES

Whom do you know to talk to about MLM?

_____

_____

_____

_____

_____

Sample MLM advertisements

These are usually to be found in the classified sections under the 'Business to Business' heading:

Absolutely a must for experienced but hungry networkers who want the biggest potential of this decade...
A serious business opportunity distributing and networking quality designer costume jewellery, no risk, free catalogue...
Change your life with this opportunity to make £250 pw part time or £950+ pw full time. Call now!...
Exceptional opportunity for MLM Marketing Directors to develop network with leading British Company...
Incredible business opportunity. We are launching two fantastic new recession-proof products in the UK and operate in £ZZ billion marketplace. MLM has created over a hundred thousand millionaires in the States alone — fact. I want to build the fastest-growing network of distributors in the UK. Phone for free video...

Real-life experience

> ### Joy Fahey, Independent Distributor/Marketing Director, working with Cabouchon Limited
>
> My career started as a professional dancer. I was classically trained and I taught dancing for more than ten years. After this, I moved to my second love, which is painting, and I put on four different art exhibitions and sold quite a few paintings.
>
> My first job in sales followed that. I worked for an estate agents, developing prospects and showing properties as part of a team. I

didn't do the negotiating. I didn't make much money and I moved over to bartending in a restaurant. I was really bumping around, in bad financial shape after a divorce and wondering what to do with myself.

A friend told me about NSA (National Safety Associates) and I attended one of their seminars. I was impressed enough to get involved. NSA is a MLM company that specialises in household air and water filtration systems and other household environmental products. I worked with NSA for a little over a year, and within three months I started to see results. Because of my teaching experience, I was also asked to help (unpaid) with their training programmes. NSA provides excellent training, by the way.

During this time I met an amazing woman, Chiquita Dumont. She told me about Petra Doring, a German woman, who was starting a direct-sales costume jewellery company. This was Cabouchon, which was started in October, 1990. I was invited to become involved, and I did, right from the start. We sell costume jewellery, priced from about £4 to about £95, with the average item selling for near £13. We produce two main catalogues a year, with two supplements in between. The concept is 'designer jewellery without designer prices'.

I am an independent distributor. When I started, I was still incredibly broke and I just started to sell, sell, sell. In the first year I had signed up about 50 people as my first-line distributors and my total group was about 2000 people. My first big cheque was £600, and that took six months. But six months later, my cheque for the month was £5000 and I made £25 000 in that whole first year, working morning, noon and night.

Last year was my second year. I now have about 5000 people in my total network, and I have more than tripled my first-year earnings in the worst year of the recession. Now I do a lot of our training, too (for which I am paid).

Sales are made directly between people and, quite often, through houseparties. These might involve 15 – 20 people and they order from the catalogue or from samples. I've been doing a few charity

53

parties. Recently I did one for the NSPCC (the children's charity) and we had about 45 people attend. I agreed to donate part of the proceeds to the charity and we raised over £300 for them in that one evening. The real beauty of this business is that it's incredibly flexible.

You might guess I'm pretty sold on MLM. To be successful, you have to have the right attitude, which I would define as 'can do'. You must be prepared to work hard. There is a tendency for people who start up in MLM to come on board with a great deal of enthusiasm, but then they plateau after a few months. It really takes about six months to get it together if you do it properly. What you need is enthusiasm and energy. The business is there, just waiting for you!

The nicest part of the business for me is to see people come into it and build up their self-esteem and confidence. It doesn't matter how old they are, who they are or what. They can come in in bad shape and have a real rags-to-riches story in an amazingly short time.

We are paid each month following for the business just done. The company takes care of all the administrative details, so it's not as though I have to set up an office with staff. However, I have retained an accountant! It's been totally mind blowing!

MULTI-LEVEL MARKETING (NETWORK MARKETING)

Rosie Ward, Sales Co-ordinator, National Safety Associates

After I left school, I was involved with horses, riding them and showing them at events. I got married and had two children and got divorced after about 15 years. Then I remarried, this time to a very successful life-insurance salesman, and we enjoyed a wonderful lifestyle. But in 1990, things went very wrong. I lost everything. We lost the house, the car, and my marriage broke up. And I was now over 50!

A friend phoned me and told me they were involved in a new and exciting business, which was NSA. I did not think it was for me. I was living in Devon at the time. But she kept calling me and eventually I tried the product out — a water filtration system. Now I was suffering from an arthritic hip at the time and was in a lot of pain. The water from the system tasted great and I started to feel better. So I became a believer, because I loved the product. I was in a terrible financial state when I started, but I turned over a wholesale volume of £12 000 worth of product in the first month and in the third month my network made sales of £27 500.

This is a people business. I recruit people by letting them look at our video. If they're interested, fine. If they're not, 'Thanks for your time.' Either they see the potential and feel right about it or they don't.

My advice to anyone contemplating network marketing is:

- Try the product and see if you like it. You have to like it, or forget it!
- Go to a business briefing meeting and see if you like it. You have to like it, or forget it!
- Be willing to work. This isn't a business for investors. It's not a get-rich-quick scheme.

Among the biggest barriers to success in this business are your own prejudices. Early on you need to identify people you know that you will contact. Some make the mistake of saying 'Oh, they wouldn't be interested', and not calling certain people. Don't be the judge.

Let them decide! Another barrier is the belief that you can reinvent the wheel. Don't waste your time. There are tried and true ways of working, and this is what we are taught. They work, very well. So why try to be different? I wasted six months trying to do it my way! Now I'm in partnership with a colleague and we're doing things right. I've been working the programme for over two years. I'm getting out of my financial mess and I love every minute of it. You meet a lot of really lovely people. It's wonderful to watch them develop. I believe this business hasn't even started yet!

Chapter 6
Retail sales

Basically retail selling means working in a shop or other emporium. Some of the people who work behind the counters of shops on the High Street or in shopping centres or malls think of themselves as salespeople. Others think of themselves as shop assistants. I think the distinction is that salespeople are more proactive, seeking out the customers' needs and pointing the way to satisfaction of those needs. A shop assistant is somebody who points to the desired product on the shelf, or goes and gets one from the back.

Another variation on retail selling is selling to the retail market, which means your customer is the store rather than the shopper in the store. This type of selling requires a good understanding of the retail environment, so it's included here.

As long as there is no incentive to *produce*, a shop-assistant mentality, which has to do more with filling requests and waiting for the tea-break, will be what you find in retailing. Contrast this with an establishment that has its people on some kind of incentive plan, where they can make more money or get some other kind of reward by selling more. Here you will find a selling mentality. If you are interested in a career in retail sales, seek out the kinds of establishment that are sales-oriented. Below are some of the choices. Underline those that might appeal as an area of work.

Typical areas

- Antiques
- Automotive, bicycles
- Books
- Cars
- Clothing
- Department stores
- DIY (Do It Yourself)

- Electrical goods
- Flowers
- Garden supplies
- Home furnishings
- Jewellery
- Music
- Office equipment
- Sporting goods
- Stationery
- Supermarkets and other food outlets
- Variety

Qualifications

- As with direct sales, usually nothing more than a 'sales personality' is needed to enter this world. In some areas, such as antiques, cars, books and music, good product knowledge is important to success.

Customers

- Individuals of all types — almost anybody

Tasks

- Being at the premises during opening hours
- Dealing with customer requests
- Explaining features and benefits of products
- Demonstrating products (in some cases)
- Dealing with service, delivery requirements
- Handling trade-ins (cars, equipment, antiques)
- Making a presentation, one-to-one
- Stocktaking (in some cases)

Compensation

- Usually lowish salary, plus (sometimes) commission
- Quite possibly straight commission on big-ticket items (eg, cars)
- Employee discounts on purchases possible

Lifestyle

- Predictable
- Probably involves evening, Saturday, maybe Sunday work
- Part-time or flexible work possible
- Modest rewards

Attributes required

- Sense of humour
- Flexibility
- Persuasiveness
- Perseverance
- Likes dealing with people

Transaction time

- Immediate (low-price, low-return areas)
- Short (high-price, high-return areas)

Whom do you know to talk to about retail selling?

_____

_____

_____

_____

MAKING IT IN SALES

Sample retailing job advertisement

Professional Sales Person

(Company, location) the UK's Premier (brand name) Motors dealership requires a salesman/woman, preferably aged between 23 and 27, to sell new/used cars.

Sales experience is not a prerequisite as training is given, but we will only consider applicants who can show an exceptional educational or career path to date or outstanding flair in their own field. As we will recruit someone of above average ability, a good education, possibly to degree level (certainly 'A' level) is essential, together with a striking appearance and extrovert personality.

Hours will sometimes be unsociable, although there is no Sunday trading, but an overriding desire to succeed, to build a solid career with OTE (on-target earnings) £35K+ and a company car will act as your vital driving force. Must be willing to live within easy driving distance of our dealership.

We are an expanding company but can only continue to do so by increasing our headcount with the right staff. If you would like us to help you develop to your full potential with the UK's most successful (brand name) dealership, and are prepared to work hard selling superb products, contact...

RETAIL SALES

Real-life experience

Annie Marchant, Wenderton Antiques

I specialise in kitchen and domestic antiques. I don't have a shop. Instead, I take a stand at the major antique fairs, such as Chelsea and Olympia in London or NEC Birmingham. Caroline Penman, who runs fairs like Chelsea and West London, got me into these more upmarket fairs from what I was doing. I participate in about a dozen a year. They usually run five to seven days.

I've been doing these kinds of fairs for about seven years now. Before this, I used to take a stall at one of the markets — Bermondsey every Friday morning and Covent Garden every Monday, for example. I did this for eight years. I've always been interested in buying and selling. I used to goof off from secretarial college and go and work in a nearby fashion boutique for nothing, just to get away from the place. I still can't type!

After secretarial training (ha), I joined Peter Robinson, which was a large women's fashion store at Oxford Circus in London. I was a management trainee, and I started out on the shop floor as a sales assistant, and did one day a week at the College of Retail Distribution. After three months, I moved into the buying department, completing my diploma nine months later. I continued in the buying office, working as a co-ordinator, for another year. Then I took off to do some travelling. I started in Italy, then Greece, and ended up working in a small hotel in Jerusalem. On trips home, I would bring bedouin dresses and jewellery and sell them through boutiques in England — there's the buying and selling again.

After a year, I returned to the UK, and my boyfriend and I ran our own antiques shop, which was really my first exposure to the antiques trade. Some time later I was back on my own again, and that's when I started trading in kitchen antiques at the markets.

I buy my stock at the same kinds of market. It's usually in pretty sad shape when I get it, so one of my jobs is to clean it up, which involves things like paint stripping, polishing and rubbing. I still encounter gadgets and devices that I've never seen before. It's very interesting trying to work out what something is for. I didn't take any formal training to develop my knowledge, but I've been specialising for so long now that I have a very good understanding of the area I'm interested in. I like these things. I'm a collector myself. In fact, I think I'll write a book about it!

To be successful, you've got to have some trading smarts — the buying and selling concept — and you need to know how to display and demonstrate things. People need to feel there's a place for an item in their kitchen, that it's usable, so a lot of what I do is about discussing how a person's kitchen works and what they are trying to accomplish.

I started on very little — about £200. These days you'd need at least £1000 and probably more. Then it's a matter of knowing that something will sell, what it is and what needs to be done to it. I love what I do. I couldn't work for someone else. I'd hate to have a shop and be tied down (plus there's a lot more overheads in a shop). I hate routine. In my job, one day you're getting up at 2 a.m. to go to Bermondsey for 3 a.m. and the next you're working some classy fair in Harrogate.

Fairs are a little like the circus. We all know each other, and look out for each other. Sometimes you have a terrible fair and very little business. That's very depressing. And sometimes it's terrific, all the right people come and you have a hit. A lot of it is luck. I'm getting ready for the *Country Living* Fair at the Design Centre in London. They had 40 000 people through there last year. I've got to start planning my display. I'm already buying stock. Then I'll do a mailing of free tickets to my customers. This business is what you make it.

Alison Kaye, Sales Representative, Kogan Page Ltd

Kogan Page is a book publisher, specialising in business books (they publish the book you are reading now). I've been working for them for three years, covering parts of London and the south-east. My job is to call on bookshops, library suppliers and other major outlets. I get paid a basic salary plus a modest commission if I meet my targets. I also get a car.

I graduated with a BA from Liverpool University. During my college days I had done some temporary work with Manpower, and they offered me a job as a sales representative when I graduated. My job was to sell our services as a provider of temporary help in the Crawley area. This was a little difficult, as Crawley had zero unemployment at the time. My training for this was basically on the job, as opposed to formal classroom sessions.

After three years I joined another recruitment company, but after just four weeks there I moved on to a confectionary distributor, Barker and Dobson, selling sweets to retailers and wholesalers. I found the job through an ad in the local newspaper. My boss at Manpower, a woman, gave me a terrible reference, depicting me as totally incompetent. The wording was so odd, it was comical. My new boss asked me what it was about, so I wrote a letter to him refuting the reference, and very soon was exceeding my sales targets. Watch out for sour grapes!

I stayed with the sweet business for 18 months. One of my clients was the large TrustHouse Forte news stand at Gatwick Airport. They told me one day that Kogan Page was looking for a sales rep in the area, and they recommended me for the job. So I was hired. I am one of seven regional reps. We sell from book covers, descriptions and our catalogue of earlier titles. One of the problems I have is the trend toward central ordering and automated systems in the really big outlets. It's leading to the McDonaldisation of the book business. It's a battle to provide input to the stores, but it's a battle I can handle.

Chapter 7
Telephone sales

A job in telephone sales will mean that you spend pretty well your entire working time on the telephone making calls and selling your wares during the conversation. It is quite likely that you will never personally meet your customers, although your business will improve considerably if you do meet them.

There are two types of telephone sales activity:

- The salespeople answer phones and take orders.
- The salespeople initiate calls to obtain orders.

The first of these will not be very highly paid, and may not even have an incentive commission schedule. The second can be very highly paid indeed, depending on what is being sold. The most money is to be made selling investments such as commodities futures contracts. Successful people in this area can make hundreds of thousands of pounds a year. The term 'telephone number salary' does not simply apply to the number of digits in the pay cheque; I think it is also suggestive of the method by which the sales are obtained.

A good film about this financial area is *Wall Street* (starring Michael Douglas and Martin and Charlie Sheen, about greed and big money). A good book is *Liar's Poker* (by Michael Lewis, about bond trading in New York and London).

Typical areas

- Stock and commodities brokers (proactive sales/order-takers)
- Advertising space and media sales (proactive sales/order-takers)
- Suppliers of business services, eg, training materials (proactive sales/order-takers)
- Mail-order catalogue-based suppliers (straight order-takers)
- Travel arrangers (eg, airlines, hotels — straight order-takers)

Qualifications

- A good telephone voice and good communications skills are paramount. Depending on what you are selling, a 'sales personality' may be all else that is needed.
- Good product knowledge is also very important to success.
- In the financial services area (brokers and dealers), you will also need qualifications such as registration or licensing as a representative of the relevant exchanges you deal on.

Customers

- In financial services, individuals with money, business people
- In advertising sales, company owners/directors, managers, advertising managers, advertising agency people
- Travellers
- Business people

Tasks

Except in 'straight order-taking' jobs
- Identifying and researching prospective customers
- Cold calling by telephone (in financial services and advertising sales)
- Responding to advertising leads
- Getting referrals
- Working a computer terminal
- Taking and entering the order (especially in financial services)
- Visiting the prospect/customer (always a good idea)
- Making a presentation, one-to-one or to a group of people

In straight 'order-taking' jobs
- Answering the phone
- Working a computer terminal
- Taking and entering the order

Compensation

- Usually straight commission
- Quite possibly lowish salary, plus (sometimes) commission or bonuses

Lifestyle

- Hard on the voice, the ears and the shoulders (slouched in a chair all day)
- Plenty of rejection (except order-takers)
- High to extremely high rewards if successful; low to zero rewards if not
- Often straight commission (but probably straight salary for order-takers)

Attributes required

- Good telephone voice
- Self-starter
- Self-confidence
- Resilience
- Ambition
- Sense of humour
- Flexibility
- Persuasiveness
- Perseverance
- Likes dealing with people
- High energy level

Transaction time

- Immediate (especially financial services and order-takers)
- Short to medium (high-price, high-return areas)

Whom do you know to talk to about telephone selling?

_____

_____

_____

_____

_____

Sample telephone sales job advertisement

> **Age 22 – 35 Articulate**
> **Business/sales background**
> **Earn £60K pa goal**
> **Foreign language speaker**
>
> If these are your personal qualities and ambitions then you almost certainly have what it takes to succeed in a sales career with (Name) Publications.
>
> As a division of one of the UK's leading publishing companies, our range of business, technology, and financial publications provides a route to high earnings in international telesales for motivated and ambitious people.
>
> If you are ready now to start a new career telephone...

Real-life experience

Stephanie Foster, Sales Executive, *Hazardous Materials Management*

I sell advertising space for a trade magazine in the environmental area. I get a good base salary and a commission of 20 per cent of the value of the advertising. I'm having a very good year, and I absolutely love my job. Prior to this, I worked for a training company, counselling people on which courses to take and signing them up. Before that I sold cars for a Nissan dealer. I enjoy the buzz you get from the selling environment.

In selling ad space, most of my initial contacts are on the phone. But actually meeting the client is crucially important to building the right sort of relationship. I attend trade shows with our own exhibit, where I get to meet many of my clients. And as a result of these contacts, it's easier to arrange a further meeting. Another way of meeting old and new clients is via seminars which we organise as a professional magazine interested in the business of the environment.

Ninety per cent of my clients are men. About one third of my clients use advertising agencies that create and place the ads. But I still find it best to get the buying decision made by the actual client. The clients really know what's going on, since they are at the front end of the business. The agency people are always less knowledgeable and are swift to make judgements, which are often wrong. Most of these ad agency people are men too, and I find them very tough to take. We're not talking major agencies here. These are mostly small one- or two-person shops. They load their conversations with sarcasm and they are so full of themselves. And on the rare occasions when I have to deal with a major, name-brand agency, I find the contact people to be mostly incompetent — very junior, and they really don't know what they are doing. So I concentrate on dealing with the clients, agency or no.

I find what makes me successful in building relationships with my clients is the fact that I always break through their wall of stress. Many of these are 'Type A' fellows, but I calm them down. One of them, always super-aggressive, became a big softy because he had a daughter my age. Now he has actually told me, 'Stephanie, when I'm busy, you're the only call I let through.' He was at our booth at a trade show recently and he took over and was actually selling space in my magazine for me as other clients dropped by.

I always try to get through to my clients on the level of their interests. A client I was talking to once was based way out in the sticks. He had placed some business with us, and we were having a conversation about getting the ad materials back to him — it was the end of the line for now. So I said, 'Well, what do you do out there for excitement when you've finished working?' 'Oh, I just sit down with my Stratocaster guitar and my Rhodes electric piano and make music!' Now I am very much into music. I have an electric keyboard and a synthesizer, and I write songs. Suddenly we had a whole new basis for conversation. Some time later he visited us at our offices and doubled his order!

Chapter 8
Business-to-business sales

This type of selling is so varied it is hard to make generalisations. What I mean by business to business is that both the vendor and the customer are businesses. The payment will usually be made by some sort of corporate enterprise or organisation, mostly on credit terms rather than by cash or credit card.

The opportunities in this field are limited only by the number and variety of organisations involved — in other words, they are unlimited.

Typical areas

Just look in the *Yellow Pages* or *The Thomson Directory*. Every field of business needs salespeople. Here are some categories that might offer inspiration:

- Agricultural equipment
- Broadcasting (radio, TV stations, equipment, production)
- Chemicals
- Construction equipment
- Distribution
- Drinks industry
- Electronics
- Energy (oil, gas, petrol, coal, electricity, solar, wind)
- Entertainment (theatre, films, music, exhibitions, venues, theme parks)
- Environmental products and services
- Financial services
  - Banking
  - Credit management/collection
  - Factoring
  - Financing
  - Insurance
  - Investments
  - Merchant banking

- Mortgages
- Relocation
- Tax management
- Food processing
- Garment and footwear manufacturing
- Hardware
- Healthcare providers and insurers
- Heating, air conditioning, plumbing
- Home furnishings and household equipment
- Hotels
- Lumber
- Manufacturing/production equipment and machinery
- Medical equipment and supplies
- Metals
- Nurserymen
- Office equipment (computers, copiers, furniture) and stationery
- Office supplies
- Paint and coatings
- Pharmaceutical products
- Plastics
- Printing and publishing (books, magazines, newspapers, directories)
- Property development
  - Commercial
  - Institutional
  - Residential
  - Surveyors
- Restaurant chains
- Services
  - Accounting
  - Advertising agencies
  - Advertising services
  - Agents (literary, creative, performance)
  - Art studios
  - Catering
  - Cleaning
  - Design
  - Employment (counsellors, headhunters, outplacement)

- Engineering
- Financial management
- Hire centres
- Information technology
- Interim management
- Management consultants
- Manufacturers' representatives
- Market research
- Meeting and conference planning
- Photographers
- Property management
- Public relations consultancy
- Shopfitters and design
- Training
- Travel arrangers
- Video production
• Sports (equipment, events)
• Telecommunications and broadcast systems
• Transportation
  - Aircraft (airliners, freighters, general aviation, military)
  - Airlines
  - Shipping, freight, courier services, removals
  - Ships
  - Vehicles (cars, trucks, buses, car rentals, taxis)
• Water authorities
• Wholesale consumer goods

Qualifications

- The more deeply you become involved in business-to-business selling, the greater must be your sales or industry experience and product knowledge.
- Some industries require professional qualifications.
- Larger organisations tend to have good training programmes.
- In many cases, these will not be entry-level jobs.

Customers

As with the business categories, your customers run the gamut from a lowly purchasing department clerk, through an office manager who is also the boss's secretary, through a middle manager, a department manager, right on up to top management and board level. It really depends on the business and the amount of money involved.

Clive Bonny has produced an excellent reference aid called *The Salesperson's Pocketbook,* available from Sales Management Partners, 8 Stonehill Close, East Sheen, London SW14 8RP, 081-876 1454. In it he lists the chain of command in business-to-business sales like this, in order of importance:

- Authority — authorises and signs off
- Recommender — approves
- Influencer — offers specialist advice
- User — hands-on implementer
- Gatekeeper — filters out supplier contact

Let's look at who these people might be in a largish organisation buying a new desk-top publishing (DTP) system for its corporate communications department, say a £20 000 investment:

- Authority — director of corporate communications
- Recommender — head of DTP
- Influencer — head of computer/information technology department
- User — DTP operators
- Gatekeeper — purchasing department executive

Now let's look at who these people might be in the case of a university buying the financing for a new £20 million dormitory and research laboratory:

- Authority — head of finance
- Recommender — faculty department head/student services head
- Influencer — finance committee
- User — estates management
- Gatekeeper — estates management

How about a company buying a 12-month advertising schedule in a magazine, say £12 000 worth?

- Authority — advertising manager/managing director (smaller companies)
- Recommender — advertising agency account manager
- Influencer — advertising agency media planner
- User — client brand/product manager
- Gatekeeper — advertising agency media planner

Tasks

Again, it's hard to generalise. Any and all of these tasks could fall your way as a business-to-business salesperson:

- Identifying, researching and qualifying prospective customers
- Cold calling by telephone
- Writing prospecting letters
- Cold calling in person
- Responding to advertising leads
- Getting referrals
- Visiting the prospect/customer
- Preparing written proposals
- Making a presentation, one-to-one
- Making a presentation to a group of people
- Negotiating deals
- Arranging finance (in some cases)

Compensation

- Sometimes straight commission, usually with a draw
- Sometimes basic salary plus bonuses
- Occasionally straight salary (avoid!)

Lifestyle

- Working in a corporate environment means that you will generally have fairly good support systems, like a sales assistant or secretarial back-up (usually shared with several of your colleagues); and reasonably good financial arrangements, such as prompt reimbursement of expenses and maybe even a regular salary!
- You will probably be given sound formal training.
- Your career will be impacted by the politics of the organisations with which you are involved.
- You will find the corporate world very competitive, certainly externally and quite possibly internally.
- Expectations of performance are quite high — people who don't come up to standards won't last long: 'First prize is a new Cadillac. Second prize is a set of steak knives. Third prize is you're fired!' *(Glengarry, Glen Ross)*
- Extensive travel may be required.
- Relocation to other areas is quite possible in a large organisation.
- You may find you need to spend time entertaining customers on an expense account (not a particularly unpleasant task!).

Attributes required

- Good communication and presentation skills
- Your personal presentation is critical:
    good clothes, good grooming, good speaking voice are all important
- Willingness to pitch in and work hard
- Technical expertise may be needed

Transaction time

- Depends on the product or service; it can range from immediate to several months, even years

Whom do you know to talk to about business-to-business selling?

_____
_____
_____
_____
_____

Sample business-to-business job advertisements

Graduates: A Career in Sales
International plc   Professional training
High rewards   Leading products
BS 5750 support

Our client is one of the largest suppliers of business communications products in the UK.

They require articulate and numerate sales personnel, educated to a minimum of A-level standard, preferably graduates, across the UK.

You will display determination, commitment and have presence to communicate at the highest levels.

You will already have two years experience in sales/marketing and be looking to develop further.

You will be given a 12-week sales and product training programme on full salary to maximise your talents.

In the first instance, contact...

Advertisement Sales Executive

If you:
- Would welcome the challenge of persuasively presenting the world's foremost international literary journal to a wide and varied marketplace
- Have experience in book publishing and marketing, and a genuine interest in the arts and literature
- Are ambitious, confident and self-motivated, with a desire to make your mark on this prestigious international publication
- Have excellent presentation skills, matched by enthusiasm, energy and a lively, self-confident personality (a second European language would be an added advantage)

Then shouldn't you be applying for this position?

Salary, bonus and benefits commensurate with the importance of this challenging position will be offered...

Real-life experience

Kate Charters, International Relations and Sales Manager, Location Specials, Reuters Television Ltd

Reuters Television is a major global television newsgathering organisation, until 1993 known as Visnews, based in London, with branches all over the world. My job is to run the department that offers camera crews, editing facilities and satellite technology to broadcasters and video production companies worldwide. I have six sales co-ordinators working with me.

The job involves some travel. Last week I was in Spain calling on several of our clients and building our relationships. A few months ago, I spent a week in Moscow. I get a good basic salary, plus a car and benefits, plus a small bonus if I hit my targets.

I joined Visnews originally seven years ago, as a marketing executive in their film library. We have a huge archive of videotape and newsreel films going back to the very beginning of motion pictures.

My job was to increase revenues from the archive through usage fees. After a short while I helped to start a new department which was producing and selling videos for the retail market — what we call 'sell-through' programming. These would be documentaries that people would buy, so they would usually have a special-interest theme... and, of course, they'd make extensive use of our archives.

Visnews Video eventually had 11 titles which we sold at retail and through direct marketing techniques. I was headhunted away from this to join Castle Communications, where my job was to sell feature films on video to the rental and sell-through markets. Each month, we'd have a couple of new rental titles and perhaps a dozen sell-throughs. My job was to come up with ways to inspire our salesforce to move the merchandise. I was also responsible for developing side deals — bartering preview exposure on the front of our films for the same thing on the front of other films. One time we worked a deal with a major theme park, Chessington World of Adventure, where we used the venue for a launch event, and carried a promotion for the park on the front of the video. Meanwhile, the park cross-promoted the video on site.

I was with Castle for a year, and then I rejoined Visnews as a sales co-ordinator in the Location Specials Department, which is the operation I now head.

Prior to Visnews I was a marketing co-ordinator with Soundcraft Electronics. We made sound-mixing equipment for recording studios. This was a terrific job. I started as assistant to the chairman, and I basically created my own job, which involved dealing with the advertising and promotional side, too.

My first job was with *Business Traveller* magazine, where I sold classified advertising over the phone. I did this for a year, coming to it from a business skills course I took. I had graduated from London University with an Honours BA in English, and I decided I'd better have some basic skills before throwing myself on the marketplace. So I did all the things I said I'd never do, like learning to type (everyone should learn to type — I've never needed a secretary!) and do shorthand, business French and so on.

I think as you go through your career, it's very important to have a mentor. I've been very lucky to have the advice of a man who worked in a PR agency I dealt with at Visnews. Over the years, just having someone to talk to as I contemplated moves or wanted to discuss career activities, has been tremendously helpful. He's always been interested in what I've been doing and very supportive. I've valued his advice most highly.

I think women often have difficulty in discussing money — I mean compensation. You have to learn to distance yourself when you ask for a rise. Don't take it personally. You should be paid what you're worth, and you shouldn't be afraid to cover the subject.

Don't get too uptight about dealing with people. Treat them as equals, and always remember, people buy people first!

Collette Murney, Corporate Sales Manager, MacEurope Ltd

I've been in sales for over 20 years. I started by working for an insurance brokerage in London, prospecting for leads. We worked in teams of two women, carrying clipboards, stopping people in the street who looked like good prospects and asking them a whole raft of questions, as in a market-research interview. By the end of the conversation, if we had qualified the person and been successful, they would know they were going to be contacted by a salesperson to discuss their insurance needs.

This was very tough work. We were paid on a per-lead basis, and if the lead led to any business, we got a small commission on that, too. The quality of the leads had to be good, or it would be game over. I did that for a year. Although it's very hard work, I would recommend a start like that to anyone contemplating a career in sales, because it very quickly cuts through all your barriers of being nervous about talking to strangers and getting to the point when the moment is right.

After a year, I went to a professional placement consultant, Clifton Donkin, to seek my next job. They said, 'You ought to be selling pharmaceuticals.' I didn't know what they were talking about. They told me a little. It's calling on doctors and hospitals with the objective of getting them to prescribe your company's drugs when they need an analgesic or antibiotic or whatever. So I went to Abbott Laboratories for an interview, and they wanted to hire me. Now I have a university background, but no degree. I was concerned about my lack of qualifications. Why should they hire me? I asked them to convince me why I should work for them, and they did. They were looking for personality and the ability to cope with the data they were going to imbue me with rather than a medical or chemistry degree.

I started in 1973, and went through an eight-week residential training programme. The first half was selling skills; the rest, product knowledge and subjects like chemistry and biology. In those days, using women as 'detail people' was fairly revolutionary. Questions were even asked in Parliament as to why young women were being used to call on GPs! The whole attitude towards sales at that time was that it wasn't really the best sort of career, especially for a woman. Abbott convinced me otherwise. I had a high starting salary, a car and an expense account. I could add about 5 per cent to my salary in bonuses by hitting my targets.

There was no prospecting involved. All the doctors in my territory were known. My job was to get in to see them and make the required presentation. We had 'detail aids', glorified flip-charts, to help us walk through the features and benefits of the drugs we were selling. I would spend the mornings talking to GPs and the afternoons visiting hospitals. Sometimes we would lay on dinners where we showed films on the latest advances in the medical area in question.

It was the culture in that business to change jobs regularly — every three or four years. I moved on to Berk Pharmaceuticals in 1976, then to two others later. One of the reasons for this is that you get bored selling one line. Changing companies gives you more variety. And you get headhunted. You could always make a better deal as you moved on.

In 1984 I left the pharmaceutical industry and went to Plessey as an area sales manager, selling telephone systems to companies. I was on a salary-plus-bonus scheme, with a car, with about half the earnings as salary. This job required a lot of prospecting. We'd work in teams, and sometimes we'd 'blitz' an area. We'd literally knock on doors and go in and see every company in the neighbourhood, finding out their needs, the names of the people to see and so on. You spend a lot of time dealing with receptionists in this mode. My advice is to cultivate them, get them on your side. A woman often wants another woman to be successful in that kind of situation, whereas men sales reps often turn on the old magic, which many receptionists find a turn off. Just be charming!

Three years later, I joined Apple Centre West London, selling computer systems. I quickly became major account manager. Pay was straight commission — a percentage of the gross profit. We had a draw against that. After a couple of years, I became publishing accounts manager, specialising in the desk-top publishing market, and in 1991 I took over the training operation, which was floundering. I came up with the idea of using government training incentives to train the unemployed in computer skills. This was a terrific programme, with our fees paid for by the local Training and Enterprise Council.

After five years, I joined MacEurope, a computer peripherals and software manufacturer as corporate sales manager. My customers are corporate end-users of things like screens, disk drives, scanners, back-up systems and so on.

Selling to the corporate market requires a lot of perseverance. One thing this business takes is time. Nobody wants to take risks in big companies, especially these days. You need to build the relationship with quality performance and quality service. You have to build trust. That's how to overcome the risk-taking barrier. If you are trusted, it lowers their sense of risk. Building trust means dealing with problems immediately, answering phone messages right away, following up, always going the extra mile. And being patient! Forcing a client into a decision will be the last deal you'll ever make with that person.

You have to believe in yourself. You have to understand the distinction between aggressiveness and assertiveness. Aggressiveness comes out of fear. Assertiveness comes out of being positive. And being positive is what it's all about.

Chapter 9

What are the compensations?

You see an ad for a sales job and it says £35K OTE. What does this mean? OTE stands for 'on-target earnings', so the ad means that if you make your targets, you should earn about £35 000 a year. Let's take a look at some typical schemes.

Straight salary

Some are paid a straight salary — usually when the job is more service oriented than sales/production oriented. In other words, if the major part of the job requires that you keep the customers happy, and it's accepted that they're going to buy a certain amount provided they *are* happy, there's not much incentive to be paid on sales results. Sales results are assumed. You may, however, earn a bonus based on customer satisfaction rather than actual sales figures.

Salary plus commission

Some are paid a basic salary plus commission. This can be a good situation, especially if the base salary is respectable. But the higher the base, the lower will be the commission payout. There's a risk/reward ratio here. Suppose a sales job should pay £24 000 OTE in a good year — £2 000 a month. That may be made up of a base salary of £12 000 and a bonus of £12 000. The bonus may be paid as earned, or it may be paid once or twice a year. Or it may be a salary of £20 000 and a bonus of up to £4 000, paid maybe once a year. See the distinction? How much does the company want to risk on you?

You may find that you get a good base pay, and then be required to produce a certain amount of sales to cover this before you start earning a bonus. For example, the salary might be £30 000 a year plus a 5 per cent commission on gross sales. However, to cover the basic salary of £30K, you first have to produce sales of £600 000 in each year. After you've done that, you earn a commission on further sales. So the results could be like this:

Gross sales	Salary	Commission	Total
<600 000	30 000	0	30 000
700 000	30 000	5 000	35 000
1 000 000	30 000	20 000	55 000
2 000 000	30 000	70 000	100 000

Straight commission

Some are paid only a commission on sales. This is true of most direct-selling and many telephone-selling jobs. In some companies, you can be paid a *draw*. This is really a loan against future commission earnings and can be based on a quite complex formula related to your earnings pattern.

Here's how it works at one life insurance company. They have what they call a financing fund. It's like a bank account. Let's assume you sell enough in your first month to produce a total commission of £900. Under their normal mechanism, let's assume this would be paid at £38 a month over two years. The company agrees to pay you up to 85 per cent of the commission right away, which would be £765 in this first month. The second month, you produce another £900 in commission and you can draw a further £765. The third month, you produce £1200 and draw down £1020. Here's how it might look over a year:

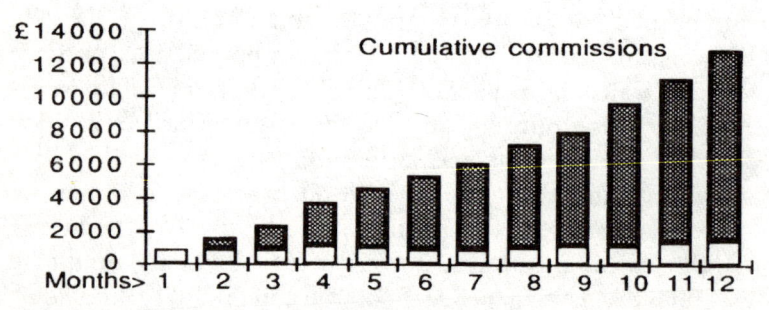

Monthly and accumulated commissions

WHAT ARE THE COMPENSATIONS?

In one year, in the example, total accumulated commissions earned are £12 700.

Now this is drawn down monthly on the basis of 85 per cent of the commission earned:

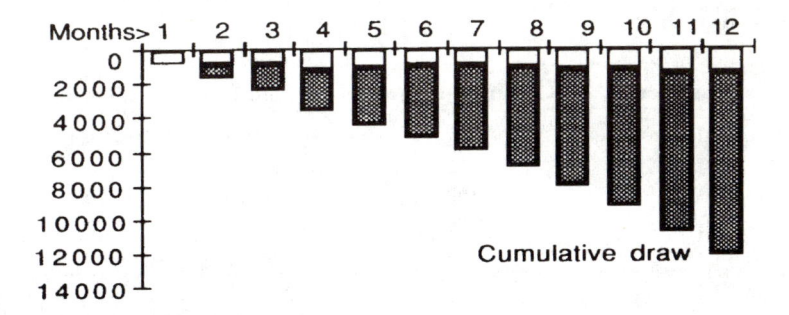

Monthly and accumulated draw

In this one year, in the example, total accumulated commission advances drawn down are £10 795.

Here are some words about this from the company's brochure:

'What happens if you hit a really lean patch? What happens if the monies aren't there in the financing fund? You've still got the mortgage to pay. The good news is you don't have to worry about interest rates. The plan is interest-free for the first five years. However, you don't have *carte blanche* to draw down against the facility. If you do encounter problems, you'll need to discuss them with your manager to see just what he or she can or cannot do to help. How you conduct your financial affairs is an integral part of your contract with the company.'

The basic concept is that the fund is to be repaid over the first five years, after which the representative is paid on straight commission as earned. The company in this case is flexible and will continue the drawdown facility, but they do charge interest after five years.

The same company has a variety of extra incentive plans for growing excellent performance. Benefits from these plans include free life insurance and membership of a series of achievement clubs. These clubs provide further benefits, such as scarves or ties, wall plaques, personalised stationery, trips to sales conferences in increasingly exotic locations, performance bonuses, more office space, and all sorts of other goodies. You take care of the company, they'll take care of you.

In some companies, commission is paid on a sliding scale, based on total performance. For example, you might see a payout table like this:

Gross sales	Commission rate	Commission	Total
100 000	5%	5 000	5 000
200 000	7%	7 000	12 000
300 000	10%	10 000	22 000
400 000	12%	12 000	34 000
500 000	15%	15 000	49 000

Note that in this plan the commissions are earned at the payout rate for the band in question. You get 5 per cent on the first £100 000. On the next £100 000, you get 7 per cent, which is added to the first 5 per cent, and so on.

Taxation

It is not the role of this book to give tax advice. Suffice it to say that different types of employment arrangements attract different types of tax liabilities. As an employee, acting under a contract of service, you are taxed through PAYE (pay as you earn) under Schedule E. As a self-employed person you will probably have a variety of business deductions to apply before calculating your profit, which is what you pay income tax on. This income would most likely be taxed under Schedule D.

Taxation laws change so often and are so complex and subject to interpretation that our advice is to seek professional advice if you have any questions. This recommendation applies equally to the areas of National Insurance contributions and Value Added Tax (VAT). The taxation of company cars is also subject to change at each Budget, so, again, seek advice if you are concerned about this.

Chapter 10
Getting ready

Head & Shoulders shampoo has an excellent advertising slogan, one that is absolutely true for you as you develop your career in sales. The line is: 'You never get a second chance to make a first impression.' Have you noticed how many of the women interviewed in this book have talked about the importance of having the right attitude to be successful in a sales career? Having this attitude starts with the way you present yourself — your own image. What you want is for the person you are seeing for the first time to carry away a positive impression of you, so that when they think of you they will immediately match that thought with positive feelings.

What helps you to build your self-confidence? It has a lot to do with the way you are turned out. When you have a smartly done hairstyle and your clothes are impeccable, don't you feel better about yourself than when you're dressed in old clothes as you prepare to clean out the attic?

When I decided to re-enter the business world, I knew it would have to be in sales and I knew the kind of job I was after. I wanted to make big money, and I concluded that I could do this in computer sales, but I knew nothing about computers. So I invested money in some really excellent clothes and a new hairdo by a top stylist. And it worked! My knowledge of computers was not an issue. How I would come across in representing the firm was.

Take a look at the successful women in the industry you are targeting. How do they look? What sort of clothes do they wear? Then model yourself after the best of these.

The importance of self-confidence

Especially in a selling job, self-confidence is essential. This has a lot to do with your own self-image. If you can feel good about yourself because of the way you are turned out, you're half way there. But the other half has to do with your own attitude about yourself — what you bring to the party; what you can contribute to the organisation you would like to work for.

I cannot overstress the importance of research as you prepare yourself for your job search. Read the trade magazines of the industry you are interested in. When you have identified target companies, get copies of their brochures and their annual reports. Study their advertising. Find out who their competitors are in the same way. Understand how your targeted company differentiates itself from its competition. Is this the sort of place where you'd like to work?

By familiarising yourself with the company, you will feel less intimidated when you have an interview. You will feel more comfortable about the company, and you will surely impress the interviewer: 'You seem to know a lot about our company', is a likely response. See how much better that is for you than you saying, 'Can you tell me what your company does?'

Another way of building your confidence is to take good training courses. The best course I ever took for that was the Merrill Lynch sales-training programme. That was an in-house activity that the company had developed and refined over the years into a course that was the envy of the financial services industry. But what if you're not employed yet? There are still plenty of courses you can take, as outlined in the next chapter.

Understand what you're worth

When I started my job search in the late 1980s, on my return to the working world after a sojourn of motherhood, I responded to several sales jobs just to see what was out there. I had not, at that moment, zeroed in on the computer industry. One of the first interviews I had was with a national newspaper. I hadn't prepared for it. The interviewer said: 'What do you suppose you're worth? How much do you think you should be earning here?'

'At least £50 000 a year!' I replied.

'I don't even make that!' replied the interviewer, who was the sales manager. 'Your OTE (on-target earnings) in the first year would be about £15 000!' Needless to say, I brought the interview to a swift close and moved on. Later, when I was asked the same question at the computer-leasing company I later joined, I gave the same answer.

'Well, I should certainly hope so. The OTE are £70K!' I was hired and went on to exceed the target by £20 000 in the first year. And I knew *nothing* about computers!

The point is, you need to get a good handle on what you think you're worth in the target job. Don't be afraid to put a financial tag on yourself. And don't be afraid to aim high. Part of your initial research should be to identify the kinds of companies that pay the kind of money you want to earn. How much do you *want* to earn? How much do you *need?* Look at your own budget. You must have an idea of the minimum money you want to make. Then add a chunk to give you some incentive, and a bit more for luck. Then find out where you can make that as a successful salesperson and go for it! The trade magazines of each industry usually do an annual salary survey. Contact the appropriate magazine and ask them if and when they publish one, and order a copy or find out where you can see one. Another way you can find out this sort of information is through networking.

The importance of networking

Networking means establishing, building and maintaining a group of contacts of people who work in your industry, or who do what you do, or who share interests with you. We've all heard of the 'old boy network'. It surely works. What about us women? Steady networking activity is a prerequisite to our success. Networking within your own industry is essential. That's how you find out what's going on. It's how you find out about salary and benefits packages within the segment, about job availabilities, business opportunities, even just ideas. It helps you to identify where you should apply your focus.

If you work for a big organisation, there's a lot of internal politics going on all the time, hence the need for a good internal network. In one job, a fellow worker advised me that the sales director was having an affair with one of the top women executives in the firm. It helps to know that sort of thing, otherwise it can be like walking in a minefield! You have to work delicately with your colleagues. You have to continuously sell yourself internally, building and maintaining your constituency.

There are informal networks — your own list of friends and business acquaintances is one such. And there are formal networks, such as trade associations and business clubs. For a comprehensive list of these, go to your public library and ask to see a copy of the *Directory of British Associations*, which will be in the reference section. For those that particularly involve women, contact the National Alliance of Women's Organisations, 279 Whitechapel Road, London E1 1BY, 071-247 7052. Examples of such organisations include:

- Co-operative Women's Guild
- National Council of Women
- Women and Training
- Women's Enterprise Development Agency
- Women's Environmental Network
- Women's Resource Centre

If you haven't really thought about it, here's how to go about building your own network. Make a list of everyone you know and group them into categories:

- Old school chums
- Former bosses
- Workmates
- Former workmates
- Neighbours
- Relatives
- Fellow commuters
- Fellow members of clubs and organisations
- People who went on courses with you
- People you met on holidays
- People who own the same kind of car as you
- People with the same kinds of dogs, cats, snakes, earwigs, etc
- Fellow collectors
- Fellow hobbyists
- Fellow customers

- People at the health club, leisure centre, job centre
- Who else?

Which of these people have you not spoken to recently? Regular contact is essential. You want to share knowledge, experiences, concerns, questions. So get going!

An important thing to remember is that *everyone* has networks. This means that whatever you do within your own network can be taken and used for you or against you in someone else's network. Likewise, if you are particularly impressed with a person and you'd like to be more involved with him or her or their activities, find out how you can become involved in their own networks.

To sum up, here are some rules of networking:

- Never burn your bridges — you need always to be able to go back to a previous client, an old employer or former colleague.
- Always look out for networking opportunities.
- Help people to build their own networks by introducing them to likely candidates.
- Don't forget there are two types of networks to work:
  - yours
  - the networks of your networks.
- Keep networking all the time:
  - phone calls: keep in touch
  - meetings
  - lunches
  - drinks
  - etc.

The importance of a mentor

Kate Charters talked about the importance of having a mentor (see page 80). I absolutely agree. You need a wise and experienced person, male or female, who can give you seasoned advice and counsel when you are contemplating an action. If you don't already have one, good sources to recruit your mentor are:

- Former business colleagues

- Former bosses (these can be very good, because they know your strengths and weaknesses)
- Former clients
- Former suppliers
- Family members (uncles, aunts, brothers, sisters)

The more familiar your mentor is with your target industry or work environment, the better. A parish priest may be great on moral issues but may not be able to help you too much on the fine points of a difficult technical sales negotiation.

Chapter 11
Training

One of the most comprehensive sources of information on the subject of training is *The Open Learning Directory*, published by Pergamon Open Learning, Headington Hill Hall, Oxford OX3 0BW (0865 773316). This lists a wide variety of courses available throughout the country. There is also *The Training Directory*, published regularly by Kogan Page. This provides a description of government measures and initiatives about training. You can find these at the public library. You'll also find copies of *Which Degree?* Interestingly, there does not appear to be a higher education programme devoted strictly to selling skills.

The library is a good place to start if you don't know where to go in your quest for training. Some libraries have a computer-aided program to help you identify appropriate courses. And they usually have brochure displays providing information about adult education programmes.

Selling skills

There are, in fact, plenty of training opportunities to learn selling skills. There are:

- Books
- Videos
- Audio cassettes
- Seminars and courses

If you feel light in this area of your experience, don't delay! Take advantage of every training opportunity by evaluating your time and financial commitment against the expected benefit from taking the training. Then, if you do undertake a programme, see it through. Don't give up unless it seems absolutely banal and insulting to your intelligence.

MAKING IT IN SALES

Books

Kogan Page publishes a whole array of books on selling skills. Here is a current list:
- *The Best Seller,* D Forbes Ley
(motivational sales techniques)
- *Cold Calling Techniques,* Stephan Schiffman
- *Conceptual Selling,* Robert Miller and Stephen Heiman
- *Empathy Selling,* Christopher J Golis
(the powerful new sales technique for the 1990s)
- *Getting Sales,* R D Smith and G Dick
(a review of sales techniques and related skills)
- *How to Increase Sales Without Leaving Your Desk,* Edmund Tirbutt
- *Inspired Selling,* J T Auer
(a book of ideas, opportunities and renewal)
- *Multi-Level Marketing,* Peter Clothier
(a practical guide to successful network selling)
- *The Sales Professional,* David Mercer
(strategies and techniques for managing the high-level sale)
- *Selling by Telephone,* Len Rogers
(tested techniques to make every call count)
- *Selling to Win,* Richard Denny
(tested techniques for closing the sale)
- *Strategic Selling,* Robert Miller and Stephen Heiman
(secrets of the complex sale)
- *The Salesperson's Timetable Planner,* Harold L Taylor
(time management for salespeople)
- *The 25 Most Common Sales Mistakes…and How to Avoid Them,* Stephan Schiffman
- *25 Top Sales Techniques,* Stephan Schiffman

Kogan Page is at 120 Pentonville Road, London N1 9JN (071-278 0433).

Videos

Probably the best known training films are those produced by

Video Arts, many featuring comedian John Cleese. Here are some of their titles:

- *The Cold Call*
- *Telesales: Your Line of Business*
- *So You Want to be a Success at Selling?*
  1. The Preparation
  2. The Presentation
  3. Difficult Customers
  4. Closing the Sale
- *The Sales Professionals* (building your client's confidence)
- *In at the Sharp End* (selling from the customer's point of view)
- *Negotiating Profitable Sales*
  1. The Preparation
  2. The Negotiation

These tapes are not easily obtainable by individuals, since they are quite expensive to rent or buy. However, they are ideal for use by a company with several employees. They are also available through some polytechnics in adult learning programmes. Video Arts hold regular screenings for potential users at preview centres around the country. Video Arts is at 68 Oxford Street, London W1N 9LA (071-637 7288).

Audiotapes

There are a number of audio cassettes available on selling skills. Kogan Page offers:

- *Multi-Level Marketing,* Peter Clothier (a practical guide to successful network selling)

Most major bookshops have a section devoted to these kinds of tape. Take a look.

Seminars and courses

Seminars on selling skills are available all over the country at various prices. For example, Spearhead Training (0295 250010) offers these courses in different locations:

Course	Length	Cost (1993) (plus VAT)
The basics of selling	2 days	£460
Introduction to selling	5 days	£895
Essential selling skills	3 days	£630
Advanced selling skills	3 days	£630
Developing selling and negotiating skills	3 days	£630

Leadership Development Limited, 495 Fulham Road, London SW6 1HH, 071-381 6233 also put on a series of courses, including the highly acclaimed *Close That Sale!* programme (billed as 'the biggest selling seminar in the history of sales training in the UK'), presented by Robin Fielder. The courses offered are:

Course	Length	Cost (1993) (plus VAT)
Professional selling skills	3 days	£725
Major account selling	3 days	£785
Telephone selling	2 days	£465
Big-ticket selling	1 day	£185
Negotiate to win	1 evening	£89
Close that sale!	1 evening	£65

What do you get in one of these? Here's an example of the content of the above three-day professional selling skills programme ('This foundation course is designed to give salespeople of all levels a complete training in the modern consultative skills demanded by today's marketplace.'):

- The 16 principles of consultative selling
- How to make appointments by telephone
- How to open the sales interview
- How to use questioning skills to uncover requirements
- How to use the LACPOMAC® selling sequence (proprietary programme)
- How to sell against competition
- How to sell an idea

TRAINING

- How to handle and prehandle objections
- How to handle 'I want to think about it'
- The importance of time management
- How to sell on your feet
- How to use body language as a sales aid
- How to develop unshakeable confidence
- How to use attitude development

TECs

Local Training and Enterprise Councils (TECs, or LECs in Scotland) have been created to help provide the country with skilled people. Each TEC is a non-profit-making private-sector company, largely funded by the Department of Employment, with a board of directors made up of top business and community leaders. There are all kinds of TEC courses throughout the country. If you don't know where your local TEC is, check with your local Jobcentre for more information (phone 0800 390000 free for the number of your nearest Jobcentre). Your local TEC will probably have a Training Help Line that can give you data on courses.

Know what you are selling

The more you know about a product or service, the more successful you will be at selling it. If the company is selling a complex product, it probably will have a training programme. For example, when I started my sales career as a trainee financial counsellor with Merrill Lynch in Boston, Massachusetts, I had to take a six-month training course which involved:

- Product knowledge — understanding the differences between stocks and bonds, investment funds, annuities and so on; the features and benefits of each and how each would fit an individual's needs.
- Regulatory requirements — to become licensed to sell financial services I had to pass tough qualifying exams set by three

entities, the New York Stock Exchange, the Chicago Board of Trade and the National Association of Securities Dealers.
- Selling skills — knowing how to prospect for business, how to qualify the prospect, how to position the product using benefits, how to overcome objections and how to close the sale.

Some years later, I wanted to sell property for an estate agent, so I had to become licensed to do this. I took a week-long course at my own expense which covered mostly the regulatory side of property sales, such as local laws, title, conveyancing matters, ethics, as well as the terminology of the business. (What's an easement? What's a right of way?) The exam was set by the state in which I worked, which at that time was New Jersey. In the UK, at the moment, there is no such licensing.

Still later, after moving to the UK, I joined the illustrious Atlantic Computers plc, a company which has since failed, taking its parent, British and Commonwealth Holdings, down with it (not my fault!). I was employed to sell computer leases to companies. I received limited formal training. I was given a couple of manufacturers' product manuals and told to familiarise myself with them, and once in a blue moon we had a one-day seminar about our lease programmes or manufacturers' product developments. The mentality at the organisation was very definitely sink or swim. Remember the golden rule: 'If at first you don't succeed, you're fired!' I succeeded, making £90 000 in my first nine months, so I was not fired. Pity! A lot of my colleagues were fired, receiving nice redundancy packages. Two weeks later, the winners who had been kept on learned that the company was dead. I received a redundancy cheque of less than £150! You can be *too* successful!

The ideal product-knowledge programme should include:

- Some historical background
- A discussion of the circumstances that led to the product's evolution
- A demonstration of how the product is made, how it is used, who uses it
- A depiction of its features and benefits

- An understanding of the competitive framework and a comparison between competitive products
- Your own product's unique selling proposition — the one feature or end-benefit that customers want that differentiates this product from all competition

Chapter 12
Finding a job

It's an extremely competitive world out there, especially these days. Fortunately, there are several ways of finding a job:

- Through advertisements
- Through your own networks
- Through employment agencies and headhunters
- Through Jobcentres (part of the Department of Employment)
- Through your own efforts, eg, mailings, prospecting, cold calling

Advertisements

The broadsheet national newspapers (such as *The Times* and *The Guardian*) have appointments sections on certain days of the week, typically Thursday. The big Sunday papers (*The Sunday Times, Observer,* etc) also have important employment sections. Some appointments sections are specialised. For example, the London *Evening Standard* has a special section on sales positions on Tuesdays and Thursdays. *The Guardian* runs similar ads on Mondays, while *The Times* does it on Wednesdays. Local newspapers tend to advertise 'local' jobs (ie, those generally not going to the trouble of relocating people to the area).

Trade magazines of the relevant industry always carry appropriate employment advertising in each issue. These are also good places to identify the headhunters that specialise in the industry.

Running your own 'position wanted' advertisement is not likely to be cost-effective, unless you have unusual skills that are in demand.

The number of people seeking any nationally advertised job can literally be in the thousands. So how are you going to make sure your application is put on the correct pile?

MAKING IT IN SALES

The covering letter and CV

Bear in mind that you have about ten seconds to make your first impression. Your covering letter should be no more than three paragraphs, plus some bullet-point highlights. Your CV should fit on one page. Everything should be immaculate, with no spelling mistakes. Certainly no erasures or white-outs. Ideally, have your letter and CV word-processed and laser printed. There are plenty of organisations that can do this for you, such as Prontaprint or Kall-Kwik on most high streets. There are also companies that specialise in creating CVs for you (you'll see them advertised near the appointments section in the major newspapers). Take a look at *Preparing Your Own CV*, by Rebecca Corfield, published by Kogan Page.

Below are examples of an effective covering letter and an

Covering letter

Dear Mr Smith

I read with interest your advertisement in The Sunday Times, 28 June 1992, for Senior Account Managers. I would like to be considered for one of these positions and I have enclosed a brief CV for your review.

I believe that I have all of the attributes demanded for a position of this calibre, for example:

- The ability to take a complex and intangible 'product' and communicate the benefits simply and concisely.

- The ability to maintain outstanding client relationships, and a belief in partnership selling.

- A track record of success in sales and marketing to major European and UK corporations, with primary contact at Finance Director or Treasury level.

- An entrepreneurial approach towards securing new business.

Although much of my sales and marketing experience comes from the financial services industry, I was highly successful in the IT sector while at ABCDE Computer Systems, Plc.

I look forward to hearing from you.

Yours sincerely

[signature]

effective CV. Note that the letter should echo key points in the advertisement. The CV is written in reverse chronological order, with the most recent events first, and so on. Under each job we have the title and a brief, bullet-point précis of the tasks or major accomplishments. Salary details should be excluded in the first instance. If you are asked to give your present salary in the initial

---

[Your name here]
Senior Sales Executive

EXPERIENCE

- Business Development Manager, **XYZ Asset & Project Finance,** Redhill, 1991 – present
  - Develop polytechnic and university finance projects — £25 million manadated business in 9 months
  - Develop private-sector finance for Housing Association projects
  - Local Authority financing

- Marketing Manager, **MNOPQ Leasing & Finance Co.,** London, 1990 – 1991
  - Big ticket asset-based finance
  - New business development

- Sales Executive, **ABCDE Computer Systems Plc,** Reading, 1988 – 1990
  - Mainframe computer-lease packaging
  - 100% club, exceeded one-year sales target in 8 months

- Principal, **NameBrand Properties,** Crawley 1980 – 88
  - Property selection, financing, acquisition, renovation, management
  - Financing and leasing negotiations
  - Town planning department negotiations
  - Historic commercial/residential properties
  - Own business, record of success and profit

- Financial Councellor, **TopRate BrokerDealer** London 1974 – 78
  - Clients: high income/net-worth individuals

EDUCATION
  Welgar College, Northampton — Bachelor of Arts, Psychology

PERSONAL
  Married, two children 14 and 9, excellent health

ADDRESS & TELPHONE

contact, put it in the letter and indicate other perks, such as a car (give the type of car as well, eg, BMW 320i) and key benefits.

The non-advertised job

A lot of jobs are not advertised in the papers. You find out about them through your networks, or you get a call from a headhunter or find them through an employment agency or the Jobcentre. (The headhunter call is not very likely in your early days, because they tend to go after people with a track record, which we assume, in the selling field, you don't have as yet.) So your initial contact may not be a letter responding to an advertisement, it may be a telephone call. Hence you must know how to be effective on the telephone:

- Speak clearly and have a smile on your face, it will come through.
- Eliminate background noise as much as possible, such as the radio, TV, barking dogs or crying babies.
- Be professional.
- Listen carefully and make notes, especially of people's names: 'What was your name again?' is not a very impressive question when you were given the name two minutes ago.
- Have an objective for the call, such as making an appointment for an interview, or having them ask you to send in your CV.
- Don't ask about details in this first call, especially 'What does it pay?' or 'What are the hours?' or 'How many weeks holiday do I get?'
- Ask if there is anything they can send you before you go in for an interview so that you can familiarise yourself more with the company — their brochure, annual report, whatever.

About agencies

Employment agencies and headhunters tend to specialise in specific industries or job titles, eg, advertising, financial directors, marketing people. Consult *The Executive Grapevine* at your local library to identify these firms, if you need to. They are compensated by the client who is seeking the employee, so there should never be a question of a fee for finding you a job. Jobcentres also are a resource for entry-level and retail-type jobs.

On the other hand, there's a variety of consulting firms advertising on the appointments pages that vaguely resemble employment agencies, but they are in fact career services firms. They will help you with general counselling on the type of job you should seek, aptitude testing, preparing your CV, self-marketing programmes and interview rehearsals. They charge fees to the employee, sometimes of several hundred pounds, depending on the tasks they perform.

Outplacement agencies perform similar counselling functions, but they are usually retained by organisations going through rationalisation programmes (ie, those making lots of people redundant) and are paid by the firm that's doing the sacking.

The targeted mailing

Perhaps you have identified a number of organisations you'd like to work for. Maybe you should do a mailing of your CV to see if there is any interest in what you have to offer. The importance of researching the company and making your letter relevant to their needs is paramount. A form letter will be treated like other bits of junk mail.

You are doing a direct-mail selling programme, and the product is you. What does it take to make it work? You have to differentiate yourself. Remember, your letter will not be the only one that lands on the desk that day. So whose desk should it land on? Find out! Get the name! Address the letter to that person. Make the first paragraph appetising enough that the rest of the letter will be read.

What is the task of the letter? To get you a job? No. It's to get you a few moments' telephone conversation that will lead to an interview. You want to generate enough interest in you so that when you call, they'll take it. Hence the importance of reaching the right person.

Think about that person's needs — the ones that you can fulfil. Make them the focus of the letter. Not 'I am very interested in working for your company', but 'You must be concerned about customer satisfaction. I may be able to help...'.

Think about what you bring to the party. If that is 'no experience', how can you make that an advantage? Is there something in your murky past that will outweigh this? Is there a parallel or an analogous situation in your career? 'Would you be interested in talking about how my experience in successfully turning around a small business could apply to your own situation?' 'Would you like to know how I achieved a 35 per cent response rate to a mailing I carried out?'

Close the letter with a call to action or an indication of next steps: 'I'll call your secretary to see if we can meet soon'.

Add on a PS for extra emphasis: 'PS Next Tuesday morning might be good for a chat, since I'll be in your building that day.'

Make sure the letter is immaculate. Double proof-read it. Eliminate all errors!

The interview

'What I look for,' said one sales-staff recruiter I spoke to, 'is tenacity, determination, personal drive and a sense of focus. I look for a feeling that the candidate is at ease with people and has very good communications skills. And I look for an overall aura of professionalism, rather than a person who is incredibly friendly and sociable.'

If you are being interviewed by a professional recruiter or headhunter, bear in mind that this is something that they do every day, so they will probably be very good at it. Here are some tips on handling the interview from Dr John Viney, UK Chairman of the executive search firm, Heidrick & Struggles International Inc (100 Piccadilly, London W1V 9FN, 071-491 3124), from his book *Career Turnaround* (written with Stephanie Jones, published by Thorsons):

- First impressions count — you won't get a second chance.

- Dress and behave as the epitome of the professional.
- Look tasteful but with a hint of individuality.
- Never lie about anything, especially your salary.
- Emphasise the strong, positive reasons for any changes in your career.
- Don't try to sell yourself too strongly.
- Don't come across as desperate — even if you are currently unemployed, give the impression that you have several irons in the fire.
- Let the consultant try to sell you the job rather than the other way around.
- Be circumspect but not off-hand; ask relevant questions.
- Be personable and try to show you have a range of interests — bring photocopies of relevant published articles or studies, and try to convey your knowledge of the market and your place in it.
- When you feel that all the relevant questions have been asked and answered, politely break off, as work is pressing; thank the consultant for the chance to discuss the opportunity.
- Be aware that competition for the opportunity will be tough.
- Prepare yourself for a meeting with the client — be entirely frank about other positions you're being considered for.

Two other books that will be helpful are *Great Answers to Tough Interview Questions* by Martin John Yate, and *Winning at Your Interview* by Michael Stevens, both published by Kogan Page.

Testing, testing

As I mentioned in Chapter 2, it's entirely possible that you will be given some psychometric tests as you go through the screening process. Psychometry is defined in my dictionary as 'the measurement of the duration, force, precision, etc, of mental processes'.

You are, no doubt, familiar with the kinds of self-awareness quizzes you see in magazines like *Cosmopolitan*. People love to do these, because they always want to know more about themselves. Psychometric testing is a lot more scientific and is used by companies to help them screen applicants for a job, and to be more successful in putting the right person in the right job than they might be if they just relied on interviews and judgement. The advantage of testing is that it puts everybody on the same level, enabling objective comparisons to be made. You won't find someone being hired purely on the basis of a test. But you will find people being rejected purely on this basis, so tests are important!

Of course, there's a book from Kogan Page on this subject: *How to Master Selection Tests,* by Mike Bryon and Sanjay Modha.

Chapter 13
Personal security

On the last Monday in July, 1986, in broad daylight and in the middle of the working day, the unthinkable happened. Suzy Lamplugh, a 25-year old, disappeared during the course of her work as an estate agent while showing a client around a house in Fulham.

Despite massive efforts by police and media there has been no trace of her and no one has any idea of what happened. Suzy's disappearance triggered an amazing public response. People identified her with their daughters, wives, girl friends, mothers and employees. The event highlighted the dangers which can confront all working people.

Subsequently, the Suzy Lamplugh Trust was formed with aims of preventing aggression at work and to help friends and relatives of missing persons.

Advice from the Suzy Lamplugh Trust

The following material is from a booklet, *Reducing the Risk*, published by The Suzy Lamplugh Trust (14 East Sheen Avenue, London SW14 8AS; 081-392 1839). The Trust is the National Charity for Personal Safety, and aims to empower all people to live safer lives — and to live life to the full. *Reducing the Risk* is relevant to all aspects of your movements and meetings while at work, and in your job search. It is included here with permission. The Trust also offers a book *Beating Aggression*, by Diana Lamplugh, that also deals with intercommunication skills, stress and tension control, and is available at £5.95 plus £1.00 postage and packing. All royalties go to the Trust which also provides education in personal safety for schools, and training in the workplace. The Trust sells a personal shriek alarm.

Here are some suggestions from the booklet, *Reducing the Risk*:

Finding a job

- Remember some jobs carry with them special risks. Assess whether you are equipped, able and prepared to cope. Choose a job to suit your personality.
- Avoid advertisements offering far too much money for very little work!
- Carefully check jobs advertised in the papers, especially if they do not give an address or company name.
- If finding a job through an agency, make sure it is reputable; that it checks out its clients, visits the premises and provides detailed job descriptions.
- Ensure that any job interview takes place at an office of either the employer or the agency.
- If, for any reason, you are asked to go elsewhere, make sure that it is in a public place. Take along a friend who can wait at a safe distance. If at all dubious, refuse to go to the interview.
- If the interview has to take place outside working hours, ask a friend to collect you at a specified time and tell your interviewer that you will be picked up.
- Always make sure that someone knows that you are being interviewed, and at what time you expect to return.
- During the interview, steer the conversation away from personal subjects that bear no relevance to the job.
- No matter how well the interview appears to be going, avoid continuing the discussion into the social scene, over dinner, drinks, etc.
- Never accept a lift home from the interviewer. Arrange your own transport beforehand.
- If you are offered a job abroad, be especially careful to check out the employer and the type of work you will be expected to do, as well as the provision of safe travel and suitable accommodation. Ensure that everyone knows your whereabouts and contract details.
- Ask prospective employers what procedures they have for protecting their staff.
- Make sure you fully understand why you are being employed.

At work avoid putting yourself at risk

- All employers have an individual responsibility to provide direction and support for their employees.
- As an employee you have an individual responsibility never to put yourself, your colleagues, clients or members of the public at unnecessary risk.
- The ideal is to have procedures and an atmosphere within the workplace where discussions about fear and other problems are seen not as marks of failure but as part of good practice.
- Learn a communication technique like assertiveness training. It makes good sense and will also help you to deal with any verbal abuse without causing further aggression. You will also learn to say 'NO'.
- Talk yourself out of problems; placate rather than provoke customers, clients or colleagues who are focusing their aggression on you.
- Study relaxation and tension control. Your feelings can escalate any aggressive situation if you are stressed or afraid.
- When you have to go out of the office, always leave details, in writing, of your expected movements; where you are going to initially, where you are going on to, and the time you expect to be back.
- Assess the potential risk of situations; avoid dangerous short cuts, walk facing the traffic on the street side of the pavement, take taxis if necessary after dark.
- Phone the office if there is ever anything you are dubious about.
- Phone in to a 'base' number if you change your plans. Always report what you are doing.
- Do not give your home telephone number or address to clients. Avoid after-hours meetings.
- If harassed by a colleague or client, tell your superiors and make sure your complaint is taken seriously.
- Wear clothes which give out the signals you intend. Humans have unwritten rules when it comes to apparel. A bikini looks good on the beach but invites trouble on the high street. We tend to expect people to 'look the part' and fit our picture of the job specification and maintain a professional

- image. You *can* choose to be different, but you need to be aware of the effect you will create — and the likely response.
- Respect other people's personal territory. Walking into someone's home can be an invasion of privacy and seem very threatening. Even taking a pen from a colleague's desk can appear aggressive.
- Keep your distance: each of us has an 'egg-shaped' personal space which we defend when we feel it is being invaded. Give everyone room to breathe.
- Do not get into a lift with anyone who makes you feel uneasy. When in doubt, use the stairs. Also *get out* if the only destination is the basement (unless that is where you intend to go, eg, for the car park). Basements can be dangerous.
- If your work entails going to people's homes, remember that the person you are visiting should ask for your credentials. Have these ready, introduce yourself, say why you have come and, if appropriate, how long you wish to stay. Do not enter a house at all if the person you have hoped to see is not there.

Be alert when out and about
- Remember, none of us is invincible — it is folly to think it will never happen to you!
- Trust your intuition: if you feel scared, or even uneasy, do not ignore the warning. Act on it straight away.
- Walk tall: keep your feet slightly apart for good balance.
- Keep your head up and your mind focused on your surroundings.
- Know where you are going and how you are going to get there.
- Look confident without appearing arrogant.
- Go to exercise classes: good posture, stamina and strength are positive aids to self-protection.

Walk away from real danger
- Defend yourself only if really necessary.
- Remember, meeting aggression with aggression adds up to confrontation.
- Your primary aim should always be to *get away*.

- It helps if you know your environment, so always be aware, alert and avoid trouble.

Backword

So there you have it. A career guide on making it in sales. Just to summarise the key points:

- First figure out if selling is for you. Take aptitude tests, talk to people who know you, see what they think.
- Look at your own background so far. Does it suggest any particular direction to aim for?
- Get a good idea of what kind of selling you'd like to do.
  - Type?
  - What?
  - Where?
  - How?
- Talk to people in that line of business. See what the job is really like. Get several opinions.
- Go to seminars, listen to tapes, read books, do everything you can to improve yourself and your skills.
- Identify the top companies in the target field and start your own campaign.
- If you really have no experience and that bothers you, try for some kind of entry-level job involving sales, preferably where there's some training given.
- The key buzzwords are:
  - Enthusiasm
  - Self-confidence
  - Attitude
  - Good people skills
  - Good communication skills
  - Unafraid of hard work
  - Perseverance
- Network, network, network!

So go out and make it happen! Good luck!

Index

Abbey Life 39
Abbott Laboratories 81
advantages of sales career 12
advertisement, business-to-business 38, 77
advertisement, direct sales 38
advertisement, MLM 52
advertisement, retail sales 60
advertisement, telephone sales 68
advertising agencies 69, 72, 75
Air India 14
antiques 57, 61–2
Apple Centre West London 82
aptitude tests 21, 107, 109–10
Arkin, Alan 35
Atlantic Computers 17, 100
audiotapes 97, 117
Auer, J T 96
Austria 15
Austrian Airlines 14
Ayles, Elizabeth 40–43

Baltimore 35
Barker and Dobson 63
Barnwell, Lisa 25
Barrett, J 21
Beating Aggression 111
Berk Pharmaceuticals 81
Bermondsey 61
Best Seller, The 96
Birmingham 40, 61
Birtchnell, Betina 39
Bonny, Clive 74
Boston 16, 99
Britain 11
British & Commonwealth Holdings 100
British Airways 25, 30
Bryon, Mike 110
Business Traveller 79
business-to-business sales 32, 71–83

Cabouchon Limited 52–4
Cadillac 76
Café Royal 25
career service firms 107
Career Turnaround 108
Castle Communications 79
Charters, Kate 78–80, 93
charts, evaluation 21–5
Chelsea 61
Chessell, Audrey 14
Chessington World of Adventure 79
Chicago Board of Trade 100
Chloride Group 30
Cleese, John 13, 97
Clifton Donkin 80
Close That Sale! 98
Clothier, Peter 45, 96, 97
Co-operative Women's Guild 92
cold calling 36, 39, 50, 66
Cold Calling Techniques 96
College of Retail Distribution 61
Collins Publishing 18
commission, straight 86
company car 42, 78, 88, 106
compensation 85–8, 90
Compleat Angler Hotel 26
Conceptual Selling 96
consultant, independent 29, 30
Corfield, Rebecca 104
Cosmopolitan 109
Country Living 62
courses 97–9
Covent Garden 61
covering letter 104, 107
Crawley 63
Cundey, Howard & Co. 40
CV 104–6, 107

Danish Embassy 39
De Vito, Danny 35

Denmark 39
Denny, Richard 96
Department of Employment 99, 103
Design Centre 62
desk-top publishing (DTP) 74
Devon 55
Dick, G 96
direct sales 32, 35–43, 86
Direct Selling Association 49
Directory of British Associations 92
door-to-door sales 32
Doring, Petra 53
Douglas, Michael 65
draw against commission 86–7
Dreyfus, Richard 35
Dumont, Chiquita 53

East Grinstead 40
Eastern Airlines 15
Empathy Selling 96
employment agencies 103, 106–7
England 26
Ethiopian Airlines 15
Europe 18
Evening Standard 103
Executive Action 21
Executive Grapevine, The 107
expense account 76
export sales 18

Fahey, Joy 52–4
Fair Trading Act *1973* 47, 48
Far East 18
Fielder, Robin 98
financial services 35, 39–40, 65, 71, 99–101
Financial Times, The 30
finding a job 103–10, 112
Florida 35
Foster, Stephanie 69–70
Frost & Sullivan 18

Gatwick Airport 63
Getting Sales 96
Glengarry, Glen Ross 35, 76

Golis, Christopher J 96
Great Answers to Tough Interview Questions 109
Greece 61
Guardian, The 103

Halfords 28
harassment 17
Harrogate 62
Hazardous Materials Management 68–70
Head & Shoulders shampoo 89
headhunter 79, 81, 103, 106–7
Heidrick & Struggles 108
Heiman, Stephen 96
Helm Financial Services 39–40
home improvements 35
Honolulu 15
houseparty sales 32
How to Increase Sales Without Leaving Your Desk 96
How to Master Selection Tests 110

Icelandair 15
ICL 30
income tax 88
Indonesia 18
Industrial Society, The 13
Inspired Selling 96
interviews 107–9
Iran Air 15
Isaacs, Ann 21
Italy 61

Jerusalem 61
Jobcentre 99, 103, 106
Jones, Stephanie 108

Kall-Kwik 104
Kaye, Alison 63
Kogan Page 21, 62–3, 95, 96, 104, 109
KPMG Peat Marwick 29

Lamplugh, Diana 111
Lamplugh, Suzy 111

INDEX

Leach, Patricia 18
Leadership Development Ltd 98
Lemmon, Jack 35
Lewis, Michael 65
Ley, D Forbes 96
Liar's Poker 65
life insurance 35, 39–40, 86
Liverpool University 63
London 15, 18, 21, 26, 40, 61, 62, 65, 74, 78, 80, 96, 97, 98
London University 79

MacEurope Ltd 80–83
mailings 107
management consultant 31
Manpower 63
Marchant, Annie 61–2
Marks & Spencer 12, 18
Marlow, Bucks 26
McDonalds 63
men, dominance of 17
mentor 93
Mercer, David 96
Merrill Lynch 16, 17, 90, 99
Miami 15
Middle East 18
Miller, Robert 96
MLM 78
Modha, Sanjay 110
Moscow 78
multi-level marketing 32, 35, 45–56
Multi-Level Marketing, A Practical Guide 45, 96, 97
Murney, Collette 80–83

National Alliance of Women's Organisations 92
National Association of Security Dealers 100
National Council of Women 92
National Safety Associates 53, 55–6
NEC Birmingham 61
negative traits evaluation 21, 24
network selling 92
networking 91–3, 103, 117

New Jersey 100
New York 15, 17, 65
New York Stock Exchange 100
Nissan 69
non-advertised jobs 106
NSPCC 54

O'Neal, Ryan 35
O'Neal, Tatum 35
Observer, The 103
Open Learning Directory, The 95
outplacement 29, 107
Oxford Circus 61

Paper Moon 35
PAYE 88
Penman, Caroline 61
Pergamon Open Learning 95
Peter Robinson 61
pharmaceuticals 81
Plessey 81
positive traits evaluation 21, 23
Preparing Your Own CV 104
product knowledge 81, 99
Prontaprint 104
property sales 35, 40–43
prospecting 36
psychometric testing 109
pyramid selling 47, 49

Raleigh 28
Reading University 30
real estate sales 35, 40–43
Reducing the Risk 111
referrals 36
Resotel 26
retail sales 32, 57–63
Reuters Television Ltd 78–80
Rhodes piano 70
Rogers, Len 96
Rowan, Cathy 29
Royal Horse Guards Hotel 26

Sales Management Partners 74
Sales Professional, The 96

Salesperson's Pocketbook, The 74
Salesperson's Timetable Planner, The 96
Schedule D, E 88
Schiffman, Stephan 96
secretarial start up 14
security, personal 111–15
self-confidence 89
Selling by Telephone 96
selling preferences 25, 27
Selling to Win 96
selling, types of
selling, ways 32
seminars 18, 97–9, 117
Shah of Iran 15
Sheen, Martin & Charlie 65
Smith, R D 96
Soundcraft Electronics 79
Southampton University 12
Spain 78
Spearhead Training 98
Stevens, Michael 109
Strategic Selling 96
Stratocaster guitar 70
Sunday Times, The 30, 103
Suzy Lamplugh Trust 111

targets, sales 28
taxation 88
Taylor & Tester 40
Taylor, Harold L 96
Teheran 15
telephone sales 12, 32, 65–70, 86
Test Your Own Aptitude 21
testing 21, 107, 109–10
Thomson Directory 71
Thomson Organisation 12
Thorsons 108
Tietjen, Tina 12
Times, The 12, 103
timesharing 35
Tin Men, The 35

Tirbutt, Edmund 96
Tokyo 15
Toys R Us 28
trade magazines 91, 103
Trading Standards Department 45
training 30, 95–101
Training and Enterprise Council 82, 99
Training Directory, The 95
Tree, Maggie 13
TrustHouse Forte 63
25 Most Common Sales Mistakes, The ... and How to Avoid Them 96
25 Top Sales Techniques 96

UK 11, 17, 26, 48, 100
USA 17, 35

value added tax (VAT) 88
Video Arts 12, 97
videotapes 96–7
Vienna 15
Viney, John 108
Visnews 78–80

Wall Street 65
Ward, Rosie 55–6
Wenderton Antiques 61–2
Western Airlines 15
Which Degree? 95
Williams, G 21
Winning at Your Interview 109
Women and Training 92
Women's Enterprise Development Agency 92
Women's Environmenntal Network 92
Women's Resource Centre 92

Yate, Martin John 109
Yellow Pages 71

Making it in
Sales